SIGNS

SUPERSTITIONS

BY
ASTRA CIELO
Author of "Fortunes and Dreams"

*"Signs, omens and predictions,
Are not all fictions,
And many facts does history cite
To prove that I am right."*
—The Mascot.

CONTENTS

CHAPTER	PAGE
I. Popular Superstitions	1
II. Wedding Superstitions	7
Lucky Periods for Marriages	11
Bridal Cake—Bridesmaids	12
Shoes and Weddings	14
III. Rings	17
Engagement and Wedding Rings	20
IV. Lucky and Unlucky Days and Seasons	23
New Year's Superstitions	29
April Fool's Day	31
Ascension Day	32
Easter Superstitions	33
St. John's Eve	35
Candlemas Day	36
St. Valentine's Day	36
Hallowe'en Customs	38
Harvest Superstitions	39
Christmas	40
V. Signs of Good or Bad Luck	43
The Sign of the Cross	46
Knocking on Wood	48
VI. Lucky and Unlucky Omens	50
Christening Customs	51
Beliefs Concerning Children	52
Beliefs Concerning Eggs	54
Charms and Amulets	59
Mascots	64
Horseshoe Lore	65
Pin Superstitions	67

CONTENTS

CHAPTER	PAGE
VII. The Influences of Mythical Beings	68
Witches	73
VIII. Signs Connected with the Body	76
Sneezing	76
Spitting	78
Moles, Teeth, Warts, etc.	80
Yawning	82
Tingling and Itching	83
Stumbling and Falling	84
Cutting Nails and Hair	86
Personal Appearance	87
Clothes Superstitions	88
On Arising	90
Squinting, Crippled, and Hunchback Persons	91
Death and Corpses	92
The Evil Eye	93
IX. Household Beliefs	95
Looking-glass Omens	96
Spilling of Salt	97
Knife Superstitions	99
Candle Superstitions	100
Concerning Ladders	101
X. Divination	102
The Mystery of Numbers	102
Lottery Numbers and Usages	104
Predictions of Wealth	106
Divination by Letters	107
Divination by Books	108
Precious Stones	110
Color Superstitions	112

CONTENTS

CHAPTER	PAGE
XI. Plant Superstitions	115
XII. Bird (and Insect) Superstitions	116
Insect Omens	118
Bees	118
XIII. Animal Portents	120
Howling of Dogs	122
Black Cats	123
XIV. Meteorological Beliefs	124
Weather Signs and Portents	125
Comets and Meteors	128
XV. Vocational Superstitions	131
Superstitions of Kings	131
Card-players' Superstitions	133
Actors' Superstitions	135
Theatre Superstitions	138
Commercial Travellers' Superstitions	139
Dressmakers' and Seamstresses' Superstitions	140
Sailors' Superstitions	141
Fishermen's Superstitions	144
Turfmen's Superstitions	145
Baseball Superstitions	147
Waiters' Superstitions	148
XVI. (Miscellaneous) Portents of Evil	150
Breaking Friendship	150
Drinking Toasts	151
Pious Ejaculations	152
XVII. Superstitions of the Orthodox Jew	155

CHAPTER I
POPULAR SUPERSTITIONS

It is an interesting question as to how the many superstitious beliefs and practices had their beginning. The origin of most of them is no doubt to be found in man's efforts to explain the phenomena of nature, and in an attempt to propitiate an angry deity and to invite a better fortune. From these sources come many of the absurd notions still in vogue among primitive people, which have been handed down in modified form to us.

Man has ever found it difficult to understand the mysteries surrounding him on all sides, and groping in the dark he has tried by prayer, incantation or peculiar practices to force nature to do his bidding.

(Superstition, therefore, arises primarily from ignorance.) Early man believed that every phenomenon of nature was the work of a spirit or devil. His intelligence could not suggest any other explanation. To this belief was added fear. The thunder, the lightning, the earthquake, darkness—all filled him with fearful dread. To him they were the workings of spiteful powers to be propitiated. Where ignorance and fear are surrounded by danger they will always grope for a way of escape. Thus superstition is born. A belief in the existence of spirits antagonistic to man gave rise to most of the old superstitions.

There is no nation, however ignorant or advanced, which does not recognize customs, rites, usages and beliefs which have their origin in superstition. The Bible speaks of such practices as had found their way from pagan sources into the monotheistic beliefs of the Israelites, calls them "abominations," and warns the Jews against them. The penalty of death was attached to sorcery, yet many of the superstitious practices continued to be observed, as is proved by the invocation by Saul of Samuel's spirit. All the prophets spoke strenuously against the existing immoral and superstitious rites, and Judaism was probably the first religion that attempted to free itself from their shackles. In Egypt, Greece and Rome, superstition gave birth to mythology with its pagan rites and ceremonies. During the Dark and Middle Ages when people were for the most part illiterate, superstition flourished with unprecedented vigor. Every religious sect gave rise to new beliefs. The

Crusades had the effect of bringing to Europe many oriental practices and ideas that in the course of time became grafted on the religious habits of the people, and not a few of them have been handed down to our own times.

It is, in fact, a difficult matter at times to draw the line between superstition and religion, for what appears as a sacred rite to one creed may appear as rank folly to the adherent of another. The Fiji Islander, for example, believes that thunder is a sign of God's anger, and he falls flat on his face and mutters an invocation to appease the deity. To an enlightened European this becomes a superstition, yet this same European may wear an amulet or charm to ward off sickness or bad luck, and the Fiji Islander might be moved to laughter at the idea.

In fact, certain superstitions had their origin in one sect trying to oppose the tenets of another sect. Again many superstitions were created by a literal or often a false interpretation of the Bible. For instance, among the Jews it was considered lucky to begin a journey on Tuesday, because in describing the third day of Creation, it is said: "God saw that it was good." On the other hand, it was thought unlucky to commence anything on

4   SIGNS, OMENS AND SUPERSTITIONS

Monday, when God omitted to say it was good. Similarly Christians have a superstition that Friday is a bad day to begin an important work, because Christ was crucified on that day. The fear of sitting down with thirteen at table had its origin in the Last Supper and its sad ending.

Many a superstition had its beginning in a command that was laid down to teach a lesson or avoid trouble. For instance, it is considered bad to step over a child. This may have had its beginning when a careful father feared that in stepping over a child one might accidentally step on it and cripple it. To drive the lesson home more effectively, it was stated that stepping over a child would stunt its growth, and in that form it is still held in respect by many at the present time. So also the belief that it is unlucky to sing before breakfast may have been taught by an indolent father who hated to have his morning slumbers disturbed by his daughter's singing, and so frightened her off by an admonition appealing to her fear. Every superstition can probably be traced to a similar cause.

There are few persons, no matter how rational or level-headed, who are not given to superstition in some form. With some there is a deep-seated belief that evil will result from an infraction of a rule. With others an amused idea that if a ceremony does no good it can do no harm, and so to be on the safe side they carry out some mummery. The lady who will not go to a card party, unless she wears some particular amulet or jewel, the man who will not speculate or play cards without first touching his lucky coin or pocket-piece, the fisherman who spits on his bait for good luck, are all descendants of the primitive savage who tried by some secret method to force nature to be good to him.

One reason why superstition has not yet died out among intelligent people is because it is contagious. In colonial days in Salem even the learned professors and lawyers believed in witchcraft. It was in the very air. Children brought up in an atmosphere of credulity rarely rise above it. It is the hardest thing to shake off superstitious prejudices. They are sucked, as it were, with our mother's milk, and become so interwoven with our thoughts that a very strong mind is required to shake them off. They become a sort of religion, semisacred in their appeal. No wonder that the lower classes cannot abandon them and that even men of intellect cling to them.

It is the object of this book to review the subject of superstition without prejudice or condemnation, but to present the data and explain their origin wherever possible, leaving it to the reader to reject such beliefs as seem absurd and irreconcilable with modern culture.

CHAPTER II
WEDDING SUPERSTITIONS

In some countries it is customary to throw money over the heads of the bride and groom as they come out of church,—it insures fortune.

In Scandinavian countries a speech is usually made at the wedding feast or a song is sung, which winds up in an unexpected crash. This sets everybody laughing and is a signal for general congratulations and good wishes.

It was formerly customary in Germany to carry old dishes outside of the door and break them in the street. If a single piece escaped demolition, it was considered a bad sign.

Sprinkling the bride with wheat is a lucky sign. It takes the place of rice in some sections. Both are considered emblems of fruitfulness.

Among the Slavs a can of beer is poured over the horse belonging to the bridegroom.

Flinging the stocking was an old custom on the bridal eve. The young men took the bride's stockings and the girls those of the groom, and threw them over their heads. If they fell upon the bride or groom to whom they belonged, the thrower was sure to be married soon.

In Yorkshire after the couple have gone away, the cook pours a kettle full of hot water on the stone before the front door in order that another wedding will soon occur from the same house.

It is considered a sign of good luck if the bride does not walk into the groom's house, but is lifted over the sill by her nearest relatives.

It is lucky for the bridesmaids to throw away a pin on the wedding day, and unlucky to be stuck with one.

In Brittany a girl who can secure the pins used to fasten the bride's dress, is sure of an early marriage.

It is considered unlucky for a pair to be married in church if there is an open grave in the churchyard.

It is unlucky to be married in green.

The wearing of orange blossoms at a wedding ensures good luck.

In the Middle Ages it was considered a bad omen if the couple met a cat, dog, lizard, serpent or hare; but to meet a wolf, spider or toad was a good sign.

It is unlucky for a bride to look into a mirror

after she is completely dressed. Some article must be put on after she is through admiring herself.

The sneezing of a cat on the eve of a wedding is a lucky omen.

A man going to be married, who meets a male acquaintance, rubs his elbow to ensure good luck.

In China, if a bethrothal is being arranged, it is postponed in case anything unlucky, such as the breaking of a vase or bowl or the loss of anything, occurs.

Among the Highlanders great care is taken that no dog runs between the couple on their way to be married.

It was formerly considered unlucky if the bride did not weep at her wedding. It portended tears later on.

/ A storm with thunder and lightning is a bad omen during a wedding ceremony.

To marry a man whose name begins with the same letter as one's own is sometimes considered unlucky.

If a younger daughter chances to get married before her older sisters, the older girls should dance at her wedding barefoot.

A clot of soot coming down a chimney at a wedding feast is a bad omen.

If the bride accidentally breaks a dish at the wedding feast it is a bad sign.

A bird dying in his cage on the day after a wedding is a bad sign. A bird sitting on the window sill chirping is a good omen.

To meet a funeral either in going or coming from a wedding is always a sign of ill fortune. If the funeral is that of a male, it means an early death for the groom; if of a woman, the bride will soon die.

It is unlucky for a woman to read the marriage service entirely through. She will never get a husband.

Bees should be informed that a wedding is in progress and their hives decorated. It brings good luck.

If at the wedding dinner an unmarried person sits between the bride and groom it means that there will soon be another wedding.

Marriages on the last day of the year are considered lucky.

Easter engagements are said to foretell money, those at Ascension, health, those at Trinity, a big family, those at Whitsuntide, peace and comfort at home.

LUCKY PERIODS FOR MARRIAGES

The notion that certain times of the year are more favorable to marriages than others, had its origin in the days of ancient Rome. The goddess Maia was not propitious to marital happiness, whereas Juno, as a good and virtuous wife of Jupiter, was the patron of happy marriages. Brides, therefore, selected June in preference to May, as their hymeneal month. For similar reasons March being dedicated to the god Mars, was not a favorable month, as disputes were apt to be the rule between the contracting parties. Every month had its good or bad influence.

Even at the present time, May is considered an unlucky month for marriages. In Oriental countries, however, May being the month of flowers, is the proper month for orange blossoms.

June is a popular month for marriages among Americans and Europeans. Some authorities believe that June's having the longest day of the year is symbolical of a long and happy marriage.

A wedding on St. Valentine's Day or other popular holiday, indicates a happy union.

Being married during a thunder storm is a sign of bad luck. If the sun shines right after a storm, the auspices are good for a happy union.

Getting married on Sunday is a sure sign of a fortunate union. Friday is a bad day on which to get married. Other days of the week are about equal in their effect upon the destinies of a married pair.

A marriage during a heavy snow-storm is considered lucky; although the contracting parties may never be wealthy, they will be happy.

An old astrological almanac gives the following as lucky days on which to be married:—

January,	2	4	11	19	21	
February,	1	3	10	19	21	
March,	3	5	12	20	23	
April,	2	4	12	20	22	
May,	2	4	12	20	23	
June,	1	3	11	19	21	
July,	1	3	12	19	21	31
August,	2	11	18	20	30	
September,	1	9	16	18	28	
October,	18	15	17	27	29	
November,	5	11	13	22	25	
December,	1	8	10	19	23	29

BRIDAL CAKES — BRIDESMAIDS

Bride cakes, or wedding cakes, are a survival of an ancient Roman custom. When a wedding was solemnized the bride and groom ate a cake of wheat or barley in the presence of ten witnesses. The crumbs were carefully preserved by the unmarried women present to insure their getting husbands.

Slices of cake passed thru the bride's wedding ring and eaten by the bridesmaids, will bring a husband within a year.

A piece of wedding cake should be put under the pillow of a maiden and if she dreams of a man, she will marry him within a year.

In some countries a plain gold ring is baked in the wedding cake and the maiden who gets the slice with the ring will have the privilege of proposing to a man of her choice.

Bridesmaids date from Anglo-Saxon times. It was the bridesmaid's duty to escort the bride to church, and it was believed that the girl on whom this honor fell would be married within a year.

A bridesmaid who stumbles on the way to the altar will die an old maid.

It is a custom for the groom to present his attendants with some gift as a souvenir of the occasion. This must be carefully preserved. If lost, the loser is apt to remain unmarried.

SHOES AND WEDDINGS

Throwing a shoe over or at a newly married couple is a custom in many countries and is supposed to bring good luck. The origin is uncertain but the shoe has been considered a symbol of authority, and as the bride has just broken from her parent's protection it is probable that the act symbolizes the breaking away from old associates. It has also been explained that it is thrown at the bridegroom in the spirit of retaliation for having carried off the bride.

It is now looked upon as an augury of luck and of long life to the bride. In an old book by Fordham we read, "He would have been content had his neighbors thrown his old shoes after him when he went home, in sign of good luck." Ben Jonson wrote in a letter, "Would I had Kemp's shoes to throw after you,—" Kemp being a man remarkable for his good fortune. John Heywood in an old play says: "Now for good luck cast an old shoe after me." Beaumont and Fletcher say in one of their comedies: "Your shoes are old, pray put 'em off and let one fling 'em after us."

In Scandinavia a shoe of the bride is thrown among the wedding guests and good luck or a speedy marriage attends the one who catches it.

In Scotland a volley of old shoes or slippers is cast at the couple for luck, but true to Scottish thrift, they are all collected again after the couple has left.

In the Isle of Man a shoe is thrown after the groom as he leaves his home on the way to be married. If by stratagem one of the bride's shoes can be taken off her feet on the way to church, it has to be ransomed by the bridegroom, who must treat the entire crowd.

Among the ancient Peruvians it used to be the custom for a prospective groom to go to the girl's house and, after gaining her father's consent, put a pair of shoes on her feet. If she consented, he led her to his home with the shoes on.

In Russia it is the custom to throw an old shoe or broken crockery for luck at the door of a newly married couple,—crockery being cheaper than leather.

In parts of Hungary it is customary on the wedding night for the groom to drink a toast to his fair lady out of her slipper.

Among the Orthodox Jews the shoe has a different marital function. A childless widow is constrained, according to the Bible, to marry her deceased husband's brother. If, however, she declines, he may give her a release. In that case she fastens the laces of his shoe and is free to marry whom she pleases.

The shoe as a symbol of a fruitful marriage is celebrated in that well-known Mother Goose rhyme:

"There was an old woman who lived in a shoe;
She had so many children she didn't know what to do."

CHAPTER III
RINGS

Rings set with certain precious stones or engraved with mystic characters were in all times supposed to influence the character and conduct of people. There are many old legends about the wonderful effect of these charms.

The ring worn by the Jewish High Priest was supposed to possess wonderful powers, given by heaven. The ring worn by Solomon gave him divine powers by which he acquired the knowledge of the laws of the universe.

The wedding ring which Joseph was supposed to have given to the Virgin Mary was an object of adoration for many ages, and many miracles were accomplished by it. It is still shown in the Cathedral of Perugia, but it seems that other churches also make claim to possessing the original. This ring, however, has been described as a very thick gold circlet, large enough to fit a man's thumb.

The power of making its wearer invisible was ascribed to the ring worn by King Gyges of Lydia, and it had also many other powers, such as bringing together long separated friends, allaying jealously, etc.

Astrological rings are worn to the present day, the stone or metal being in conformity with the signs of the planets, and thus bringing luck to the wearer.

Rings are often used for divination. A number of rings, each inscribed with a name, are thrown into a bag, and one drawn at random. The answer to any question is thus given.

Rings are considered a preventive of many diseases. For the cure of croup an amber ring is often worn. For cramp and abdominal pains, a ring made of a coffin nail is supposed to be efficacious. For rheumatism, a copper ring, or one of copper and zinc welded together, is thought to have curative powers.

Marcellus, an old Roman physician, prescribed for a pain in the side, a gold ring inscribed with certain Greek characters and worn on the hand of the side opposite the pain. Trallian, another ancient doctor, cured colic and bilious complaints by an octangular ring of iron on which he engraved a message to the disease to leave the body.

Rings on which were engraved the names of three kings of Cologne were considered efficacious in the cure of various disorders. On them were also engraved the words, "God is a remedy."

For sore eyes, a plain gold wedding ring is considered a sovereign remedy to this day.

A ring made of a silver coin, taken from a beggar, is supposed to be a cure for epilepsy.

Among the peasantry of France, before a couple are wed, a ring of iron is put on the forefinger of the bride. It is usually made of a nail of a horseshoe. In certain parts a ring of straw is used. These are first blessed by the priest and insure a happy life.

In Russia, in order to discover which girl of a village shall be married first, each places a ring in a little heap of corn on the barn floor. A rooster is then let loose among the corn. He pecks at the grains until one ring is exposed. The owner will be married before her companions.

In Sweden girls hide under teacups or kitchen pots a ring, a coin and a piece of black ribbon. If the ring comes to light first, the owner will marry, if the coin, she will get a rich husband, but if the ribbon, she will die an old maid.

To find a ring is a sign of good luck if it be gold, of peace of mind if it be silver, but of trouble, if it be brass.

ENGAGEMENT AND WEDDING RINGS

Rings have figured prominently in marriages from prehistoric times, and many superstitions cling to them. It is not strange that a rite that is fraught with such serious results to the conracting parties should have awakened a sense of dread and a desire to foretell the future by speculation and divination.

Among some peoples instead of exchanging rings a piece of gold or money is broken in halves, each party keeping a half. To lose one's half is considered very unlucky.

An engagement ring is supposed to be:
is a harbinger of luck and happiness.

An engagement ring with the bride's birthstone
"A contract of eternal bond of love,
Confirmed by mutual joinder of your hands."

Formerly men wore engagement rings as well as women, but in the course of time left them off as being a sign of bondage.

A diamond engagement ring is especially lucky, as diamonds are considered the highest form of gift, and the sparkle is supposed to originate in the fires of love.

A pearl in a ring is unlucky, as pearls signify tears.

To lose a stone out of an engagement ring foretells bad luck, unless it is replaced before the wedding takes place.

During the Commonwealth in England, the Puritans tried to abolish wedding rings as being a remnant of heathen practice.

The ring, being round and without end, is a symbol of never-ending love and affection that should continue to flow in an uninterrupted circle.

If a wedding ring breaks, it is a sign of marital trouble.

A wedding ring that has been worn to a thin thread is lucky and brings luck to the wearer's children.

The wedding ring is usually worn on the fourth finger of the left hand. The probable reason is that the left hand is not used as much as the right and the fourth finger is rarely used alone.

It was formerly believed that a special artery led from the heart to the fourth finger.

Among Orientals the ring is usually worn on the index finger of the left hand, which is called the lucky finger.

A wedding ring rubbed three times on the eye is supposed to be a cure for styes.

A wedding ring should be turned around three times if you want your wish to come true.

It is unlucky to take off your wedding ring except in cases of necessity.

CHAPTER IV
LUCKY AND UNLUCKY DAYS AND SEASONS

The belief that some days bring luck and others the opposite, is prevalent the world over and has its origin in astrology. Few intelligent people are free from this superstition.

If a person has had luck on a certain day, three times in succession, it is safe to assume that it is his lucky day and any business undertaken on that day will prove successful. Conversely, if a day has shown itself unfortunate, business or travelling should be avoided on that day.

A day that is good for one person may be correspondingly unlucky for another. What is one man's food is another man's poison.

Religious persons believe that the last Monday in December is unlucky for serious matters, as Jesus was betrayed on that day.

Friday is generally considered unlucky for any new undertaking, because Jesus was crucified on that day.

If Friday falls on the thirteenth of any month, it is doubly unlucky for business or speculation.

John Gibbons, an eminent scientist considered Friday an unusually lucky day. He was born, christened and married on that day and was fortunate in all of his undertakings.

To move into a new home on Friday is unlucky. Monday and Wednesday are particularly fortunate.

To be born on the 29th of February, leap year, is considered lucky and the person will be successful as a speculator.

An old verse says:

"There are days of which the careful heed,
When enterprise will sure succeed."

Books on astrology give the following as unlucky days:

January,	1	2	4	5	10	15	17	29
February,	8	10	17	26	27	28		
March,	16	17	20					
April,	7	8	10	16	20	21		
May,	3	6	7	15	20			
June,	4	8	10	22				
July,	15	21						
August,	1	9	20	29	30			
September,	3	4	6	7	21	23		

October, 4 6 16 24
November, 5 6 15 20 29 30
December, 6 7 9 15 22

Never undertake any important business on a day that has brought you any misfortune or calamity.

According to old astrologers, six days are perilous to sick persons, and it is not safe to let blood on these days. They are January 3, July 1, October 2, April 30, August 1, and December 31.

Thursday in May was never to be regarded as a holy day, according to an ancient church authority.

No vines are to be planted during leap year, as they will not thrive.

An old missal gives the following predictions regarding certain days of the year:

January—
  Of this first month the opening day
  And seventh like a sword will slay.
February—
  The third day bringeth down to death,
  The fourth will stop a strong man's breath.
March—
  The first the greedy glutton slays,
  The fourth cuts short the drunkard's days.

April—
   The tenth day and the eleventh too,
   Are ready death's fell work to do.
May—
   The third to slay poor men had power,
   The seventh destroyeth in an hour.
June—
   The tenth a pallid visage shows,
   No faith nor truce the fifteenth knows.
July—
   The thirteenth is a fatal day,
   The tenth alike will mortals slay.
August—
   The first kills strong men at a blow,
   The second lays a cohort low.
September—
   The third day of the month September
   And tenth bring evil to each member.
October—
   The third and tenth with poisoned breath
   To men are foes as foul as death.
November—
   The fifth bears scorpion stings of pain,
   The third comes with distraction's train.
December—
   The seventh is bad for human life,
   The tenth with serpent's sting is rife.

"The lucky have whole days in which to choose,
The unlucky have but hours, and these they lose."

Sunday is a pun day, Monday's a dun day, Tuesday's a news day, Wednesday's a friend's day, Thursday's a cursed day, Friday's a dry day, Saturday's the latter day.

Born on Monday, fair of face; born on Tuesday, full of grace; born on Wednesday, sour and sad; born on Thursday, merry and glad; born on Friday, worthily given; born on Saturday, work hard for your living. Born on Sunday, you'll never know want.

The day of the week on which the 3rd of May falls is unlucky for taking an account of cattle on a farm. St. Stephen's day is unlucky for bleeding horses.

The Spanish have a proverb which says: Don't wed, don't go aboard a ship and don't leave your wife on Thursday.

According to a Spanish belief, Saturday always is sunny and therefore lucky. Wednesday in Passion Week is always rainy and therefore unlucky. On that day it is said that Peter went out and wept, hence heaven sends rain to commemorate his tears.

28 SIGNS, OMENS AND SUPERSTITIONS

An Italian belief fixes Tuesday and Friday as unlucky days for a voyage and for a marriage.

The Japanese have designated five days of the year as unlucky, and in order to avert their bad influence have made them the days of great festivals. (It is customary to wish one another happiness on those days in order to oppose their otherwise unhappy effects. They never begin a journey on an inauspicious day and there is a printed table in all their roadhouses and inns, showing what days of the month are unfavorable for travel.

The French regard Sunday as a very lucky day for all enterprises.

According to an old Hebraic tradition, the sun always shines on Wednesday, for according to the Bible, it was created on that day. Therefore, it is a good day for any enterprise.

The 14th of April, 1360, was called "Black Monday." King Edward III with his army lay before Paris and the day was so dark, cold and unhealthy that many soldiers died from exposure and were frozen on the backs of their horses. This day was commemorated in England for many years.

The Turks consider the 13th, 14th and 15th

of each month as lucky days to transact business and go on a voyage.

It is considered unlucky to take a trip immediately after hearing of the death of a friend.

In certain parts of England, Tuesday and Wednesday are lucky days. It is thought unlucky to turn a feather bed or mattress on Sunday.

A Scotchman rarely begins anything on the day of the week on which May 3rd falls. He calls it the "Dismal Day."

Among the Hindoos, Monday is considered a lucky day for a trip. Sunday is lucky for sowing seed or beginning a building. Tuesday is lucky for soldiers in battle. Wednesday is a lucky day for merchants and good for collecting debts. Thursday is good for beginning a new business. Friday is lucky for the making of friends and the wearing of new garments. Saturday is unlucky, as it excites quarrels.

NEW YEAR'S SUPERSTITIONS

The first day of the year is naturally a day of importance as its events may have a tendency to affect all the days that are to follow. Many a strange belief, therefore, centres about this day in all lands, and the symbols of future good or bad luck are eagerly sought in everything that occurs.

In many parts of England it is believed that if a male person crosses the threshold first, it betokens good luck, whereas, if a female be the first to cross, bad luck is sure to follow. A man or boy, therefore, is often hired to enter a house before the occupants are up. Whole bands of males are employed for a small fee, for this purpose.

If a clergyman be the first to enter a home on New Year's Day the significance is good.

Chimneys used to be cleaned on New Year's Day in England, so that luck could descend and remain all the year.

It was considered luckier for a dark-haired man than for a fair-haired man to be the first to enter a home. A bachelor was luckier than a married man. A widower brought bad luck.

It is customary in some parts for the first visitor to bring a gift of a cake or loaf of bread, to indicate prosperity for the rest of the year.

It is considered unlucky to remove anything from a house on New Year's Day, until something has been brought in from without. Each visitor therefore brings a slight gift.

Eating a cake is considered a sure bringer of luck on the first of the year. In rural districts, special New Year cakes are baked for this purpose.

To lend something to a friend is sure to bring a good return.

To put on new clothes on New Year is considered lucky, so also to bathe.

Money earned on New Year's Day will bring a hundredfold in its train.

Resolutions made on New Year's day should be carried out, if they are good, and will insure good luck.

It is good to give alms on the New Year. In many parts poor folks are invited to partake of the family's cheer.

APRIL FOOL'S DAY

The first of April was celebrated among the ancients as the beginning of the vernal equinox amid general frolicking, and from that is derived our own April Fool's Day. It is customary to send people upon foolish errands and make them appear ridiculous.

The celebration of this day is world wide. Even in pagan India the people join in the fun.

In Mohammedan countries the highest castes vie with each other in playing practical jokes.

To be fooled by a pretty girl denotes that you will marry the girl if you are single, or befriend her if already married.

To lose your temper when sent on a fool's errand, means bad luck.

To get married on April Fool's Day means that the lady will wear the breeches and the man play second fiddle.

Children born on this day will be lucky in legitimate business but unlucky in speculation.

ASCENSION DAY

This day commemorates the ascension of the Savior into heaven and is the occasion of many superstitions.

To work on this day, especially in underground quarries or mines, is considered unlucky in Catholic countries, and even in England underground work is suspended from dawn to dusk.

Wells and reservoirs are decorated with flowers to insure pure water during the year.

To fall or stumble is particularly unlucky, and means a loss of health or money. An ancient way

SIGNS, OMENS AND SUPERSTITIONS

of preventing disaster if you have fallen is to lie flat on the ground and say:

"Raise me up and comfort me, Angel of Mercy."

Alms given to a blind or lame man on this day will come back a hundredfold.

Begin the day by giving away a coin, however small. It will bring you an unexpected fortune within the year.

EASTER SUPERSTITIONS

Easter commemorates the resurrection of the Savior from the dead, and in all countries it is celebrated with peculiar rites and ceremonies.

"Lifting" is an old custom that is supposed to illustrate the rising from the grave. Men and women would visit each other, and go through the following practice. A person would lie flat upon his back. Four others would take hold of him, one at each leg and arm and lift him up three times. There is a belief that if the recumbent person holds his breath, he can be lifted by the little finger of each of the four lifters.

Girls were often put into a chair and lifted by boys who claimed a kiss for their trouble. This was also called "heaving."

Easter eggs had their origin in the belief that

34 SIGNS, OMENS AND SUPERSTITIONS

the egg was a symbol of the Resurrection. Some attribute their origin to their symbolizing Spring. Dyeing eggs in lively colors was a token of joy or gayety. Red dye was taken as a symbol of Christ's blood.

Eggs are often blessed on Easter before being eaten. They then keep away bodily ailments.

To win an egg by "picking" brings good luck. It is a popular game with boys.

To find two yokes in an Easter egg foretells a great gain in wealth.

To refuse to eat an Easter egg, if offered by a friend, signifies a loss of friendship.

Rabbits are supposed to lay eggs on Easter. This is an old Teutonic belief.

Among the more popular Easter pastimes are rolling eggs down hill and finding hidden eggs. Both are considered lucky ceremonies.

It is considered lucky to plant garden seed and potatoes on Good Friday.

Good Friday is the best day in the year for weaning babies.

It is a sign of luck to break pottery on Good Friday. It will save the house from damage during the rest of the year.

ST. JOHN'S EVE.

This is a popular day in England and Ireland and many a superstition is connected with it.

Bonfires are built in memory of the ancient druids, and children dance around them. To jump over a bonfire insures luck for the next harvest.

While looking into the fire, the men throw pieces of wheaten cake over their shoulders, saying:

"This I give thee to preserve my horses, or my sheep." This is supposed to propitiate the Biblical idol, Baal.

When a Scotchman goes to bathe or drink at a fountain or well on this day, he always approaches by going around the spot from east to west on the south side, in imitation of the motion of the sun. This is called "going around the lucky way."

Dancing around a fire propitiates the forces of evil. It is also a demonstration of joy and a plea for good luck.

Watch the flames and if you see a familiar face therein, beware of that person, as he will harm you.

CANDLEMAS DAY

This day is celebrated in Christian countries as the day of the "Purification of the Virgin." It had its origin in Roman times in honor of the goddess Februa, after whom February was named.

Every pious Catholic goes to church on that day with a lighted candle in supplication to "Our Lady" for success in household affairs.

In many parts of England the day is connected with the collection of rents and leases are still made out beginning with Candlemas Day.

The agent of an estate comes at midnight and knocks at the door of his tenant. "I come," he cries, "to demand my lord's just dues: eight groats and a penny, a loaf of bread, a cheese, a collar of brawn and a jack of beer. God save the King and the Lord of the manor."

To pay rent on Candlemas Day insures freedom from debt for the year.

To light a candle dedicated to one's saint, brings good luck.

ST. VALENTINE'S DAY

St. Valentine was a Christian bishop who suffered martyrdom in 270 A. D. on February 14th. He was later ordained the patron saint of true

SIGNS, OMENS AND SUPERSTITIONS

love. Maids and youths were accustomed to become engaged on that day in his honor.

Sending verses and picture cards to one's best beloved has become a popular pastime in England and America on Valentine Day. A girl who fails to receive a remembrance from some swain is doomed to die an old maid.

Says an old Valentine verse:

"When I go out, the first swain I see,
In spite of fortune shall my true love be."

On the eve of Valentine's Day it was the custom for a man to get five bay leaves, pin four of them to the corners of his pillow and the fifth in the centre, and then go to sleep. If he dreamed of a girl, he would marry her before the year was out.

Another custom was to write your friends' names on pieces of paper, roll them in clay and throw them into a dish of water. The first paper that floated up indicated the one you would marry.

If you expect a visit from your true love on that day, keep your eyes shut till he comes. If you see another man first, it may mean a loss of the other's love.

To be married on Valentine's Day betokens happiness and success.

HALLOWE'EN CUSTOMS

Christian history has given us this day as sacred to all saints. In most countries there are curious rites and ceremonies connected with it.

In Catholic lands it is a day of prayer and the people visit the churchyards and pray to the saints and to the departed of their families for success and for forgiveness of sins. In Protestant countries the day is given over to merriment.

Hallowe'en was originally a day for remembering the dead. Ghosts and spirits are supposed to wander abroad at night.

Witches and demons make the night their own, and woe to the person they catch after dark.

Spectres made of pumpkins and sheets are used both to frighten men and to scare off evil spirits.

To see your shadow cast by the moon is distinctly unlucky.

It is a time full of portents, and there are various ways of divining the name of one's future sweetheart.

Place two nuts in the fire side by side. If they burst and fly apart it betokens bad luck and

SIGNS, OMENS AND SUPERSTITIONS

a separation. If they burn up together, it is a good omen, and means a happy marriage.

Pare an apple so that the peel remains in one long piece. Swing this around your head three times and throw it on the floor. The letter it forms will be the initial of your sweetheart's name.

Walk backwards, looking into a mirror. The first man or maid whose reflection you see, will marry you.

To find two kernels in an almond on Hallowe'en's night is particularly lucky and means marriage within a month.

HARVEST SUPERSTITIONS

In ancient times, when the owners of land had gathered in their harvest, they feasted with their servants who helped till the ground. This idea has been perpetuated in our day in agricultural countries. Harvest Home is celebrated in most agricultural countries. In England it partakes of some of the aspects of Thanksgiving Day.

The "Kern Baby" is much in evidence in these festivities. It is an image dressed up and decorated with corn or wheat and carried before the reapers as a sign of luck.

In some places a big doll dressed up in tinsel with a sheaf of wheat under its arm is placed on a pole and the harvest hands dance around it, rejoicing.

Sometimes a real girl is dressed up in a robe of wheat and is paraded around the field for luck. A corn supper in which all partake winds up the festivities.

A special prayer to one's favorite saint is usual before the harvest, to insure good weather till the wheat is all garnered.

In Catholic countries, the first wheat garnered is shaped into a cross which is hung in front of the granary for good luck.

A red ear of corn is considered a lucky find. It should be carefully preserved until the next harvest.

An ear of corn with seven or fourteen rows is especially lucky and betokens a good harvest.

CHRISTMAS

A festival corresponding to Christmas was held in Rome in honor of Bacchus, but with the advent of Christianity it changed its character and was solemnized to celebrate the birth of Christ.

SIGNS, OMENS AND SUPERSTITIONS

Many of the old pagan rites and superstitions still remain.

Mistletoe was held in high esteem by the druids and regarded with religious superstition. They used it in their incantations. It is used for decorating during Christmas, and is usually hung from the chandeliers.

A girl standing under a piece of mistletoe may be kissed by any man who finds her there. If she refuses to be kissed, she invites bad luck. If she be kissed seven times in one day, she will marry one of the lucky fellows within a year.

In olden days mistletoe was laid on the altars in churches as an emblem of the grace of the Savior, and betokened a prosperous year.

In York, England, mistletoe is laid upon the altar of the cathedral and the priest proclaims freedom to all wicked souls.

Evergreen leaves and boughs are also a relic of paganism, and are supposed to bring cheer and luck.

The Christmas tree is a survival of northern mythology and was first made popular in Scandinavian countries when they adopted Christianity. It symbolizes the ever green and abiding power of salvation.

Christmas candles probably had their origin in the Jewish festival of lights (Chanuca), which occurs at the same time. Lights are lit for seven days to commemorate the victories of the Maccabbees.

Yule logs are large logs of wood that are thrown into the grate to make the Christmas eve more festive. The flame is supposed to keep out evil influences. Christmas candles serve the same end.

To see a familiar face in the blaze of a yule log, betokens an early marriage with the person thus seen.

To become engaged on Christmas eve, is a sure sign of a happy married life.

A child born on Christmas day will be free from care and very lucky.

St. Nicholas, or Santa Claus is the patron saint of Christmas. He is supposed to come down the chimney with his pack on his back and distribute toys and gifts to old and young. The only way to secure his favor is to be good and obedient.

Kris Kringle is another name for Santa Claus. It is derived from the German "Krist Kindli" or Christ Child. He is represented as entering homes and making children happy on the "Holy Night."

CHAPTER V
SIGNS OF GOOD OR BAD LUCK

"Good and ill luck," says the French philosopher, Montaigne, "are in my opinion sovereign powers. It is absurd to think that human prudence is able to act the same part as Fortune will do." Shakespeare says:

"There's a divinity that shapes our ends,
Rough-hew them how will will."

The belief in the power of some object or some act to produce a change in one's fortunes for better or for worse, is inherent in the human race. There are few words in our language that have such a universal application as LUCK. The man who believes in nothing else, believes in luck and performs some mummery to propitiate the goddess of Fortune, who moves in such mysterious ways to perform her deeds.

Luck may be defined as chance, or if a man be religious, as Providence. Among the ancients, Fortuna was depicted as a blindfolded woman with a horn of plenty, or with a wheel as an emblem of instability and chance.

The Romans had a habit of casting into an urn a stone every day, the color of the stone denoting whether the person was in good or bad luck. At the end of the year the stones were counted and a balance cast to see whether good or bad preponderated.

It is unlucky to be recalled after starting away on a voyage. At least a day should be allowed to elapse before starting out again.

To leave home and be compelled to come back for some article which was forgotten, is unlucky, unless you sit down for a moment before going out a second time.

Carrying a crust of bread in one's pocket is considered lucky and brings prosperity.

If in eating you miss your mouth and the food falls, it is unlucky and denotes illness.

A bent coin or one with a hole in it, are often carried for good luck. A crooked sixpence is popular for this purpose in England.

In many rural districts it is customary to give back to a customer of corn or cattle a small part of the money he has just paid. This is called "luck money."

In some countries the buyer gives the seller a small coin to insure his luck.

SIGNS, OMENS AND SUPERSTITIONS

To count your gains is supposed to bring bad luck. To reckon on money you are to receive and lay out plans of spending it, is considered unlucky. One should never count one's chickens before they are hatched.

Burning tea leaves is supposed to bring good luck, but to burn the leaves of a rose is a bad omen.

Finding a four-leaf clover is a sure sign of good luck. It should be worn in the lapel or pinned to one's coat.

There is a legend that Eve on being ejected from Paradise took a four-leaf clover with her.

To pluck an ash leaf was considered lucky in olden times.

On meeting a person out on new business, it is well to salute him with "I wish you good luck."

It is bad luck to shake hands with any one across the table.

It is a bad omen to find the bellows on the dining table.

It is a sign of ill luck to find money and not spend it. It should be spent in a good cause, or given in charity.

"See a pin and pick it up, all the day you'll have good luck.
See a pin and leave it lay, you will have bad luck all the day."

It is lucky to throw a small coin into a well of drinking water.

To sit crosslegged is considered a sign of good luck. To cross one's fingers is another way of averting evil.

THE SIGN OF THE CROSS

The Cross, the emblem of Christianity, has served many superstitions. It is a bringer of good luck and wards off evil.

Contrary to the generally accepted belief, the Cross did not have its origin as a religious emblem in Christianity. The Indians, when Columbus first landed, had similar devices. Cortez found the cross universally adored by the Aztecs, and this led the Spanish priests to claim that the devil had given it to them in order to damn them with a false religion. The Hindoos, too, had a cross among their religious symbols.

Making the sign of the cross at rising or lying down, at going out or coming in, at lighting of candles or closing of windows, etc., is considered a pious and profitable ceremony.

An old church writer says:

"At the delivery of the bread and wine of the sacrament, the worshippers flourish with their thumbs like making the sign of the cross. They also do it when coming to church or saying their prayers."

In Spain, "no woman goes in a coach or travels without crossing herself. It keeps away evil and ensures a safe trip."

In Catholic countries, signposts and even tavern signs bear a cross as a sign of good luck.

In some countries when a woman milks a cow she dips her finger in the milk with which she crosses the cow, muttering a prayer. This will make the milk flow freely.

Easter buns are marked with a cross as a sign of faith.

To hold up a crucifix, or anything resembling a cross was the surest way of defeating the devil. In "Faust," Valentine drives off Mephistofeles by holding up the cross-shaped hilt of his sword.

During a thunder storm or in the face of sudden danger, make the sign of the cross on your forehead or breast.

48 SIGNS, OMENS AND SUPERSTITIONS

To cross one's fingers during a game of chance, brings luck, and the reverse to your opponent.

To dream of a cross is a sign of good fortune to follow shortly.

To cross knives or forks at table is a sign of bad luck.

In Sicily a bandit will not attack his victim without first crossing himself and praying to his favorite saint for protection.

KNOCKING ON WOOD

One of the most prevalent customs, indulged in by men of science as well as the illiterate man in the slums, is by touching or knocking on wood to ward off evil or prevent disappointment. Its origin is very much in doubt. Some attribute it to the ancient religious rite of touching a crucifix when taking an oath. It is also ascribed to the beads of a rosary touched in prayer. Among the ignorant peasants of Europe it may have had its beginning in the habit of knocking loudly to keep out evil spirits. Its introduction into this country seems to have been of recent date, but it has become well-nigh universal; even a president of the United States is accused of resorting to it.

To brag about good health or success, according to the general belief, invites the envy of the powers of evil, and to counteract this you must, according to some authorities, touch wood; while according to other wisacres, you should knock on wood three times.

Charms made of wood are often worn on watch chains so that the wearer may have an article handy for the purpose.

From this practice other superstitions have originated. A well-known financier always plays with his massive gold watch chain in the belief that the touch of gold will insure success.

Sir Walter Scott, while a student at college, always fumbled with a wooden button which was attached to his coat. This brought him success in his recitations. It is related that when his fellow students secretly cut off the button, he was so flustered on discovering its absence, that he failed hopelessly and was sent to the tail end of his class.

CHAPTER VI
LUCKY AND UNLUCKY OMENS

"She that pricks bread with fork or knife, will never be a happy wife."

"Mend your clothes upon your back, sure you are to come to wrack."

It is unlucky to use elder wood or evergreen to make a fire.

To find an old flint arrow is considered lucky.

To find nine peas in a pod is a forerunner of luck.

The extreme tip of a calf's tongue, dried and carried in the pocket, will insure having some money always in your purse.

A luck-stone, with a hole in it, is sure to bring luck.

Four persons shaking hands in crosswise fashion, foretell a coming marriage.

Two bells ringing in the house at one time foretell a parting. So also does a hollow cavity in a fresh-cut cake and a loaf that breaks in two while being cut.

To enter a house with the left foot first brings bad luck to the occupants.

CHRISTENING CUSTOMS

Christening, as the name indicates, is a ceremony which has for its object the consecrating of a child to the service of Christ, and starting him on his career as a Christian. It had its origin in the rites of John the Baptist, who belonged to a sect that believed that immersion in water would wash away all sins and prepare the neophyte for the Kingdom of God, which was supposed to be near at hand.

In the middle ages a child was usually presented by its godparents with silver or gold spoons. A rich sponsor often gave a set of twelve spoons, one for each of the disciples. Less wealthy people gave one or more spoons. These were considered lucky and induced the child to lead a virtuous life.

The phrase "born with a silver spoon in its mouth," arose from this custom.

A silver cup is often given and the child that drinks from it is supposed to drink happiness during its life.

The gift of coral and amber in the form of

a chain or charm to a new-born baby is also believed to bring good luck. Coral is supposed to be a defense against "Fascination" or witchcraft. Amber keeps away infectious diseases.

A Sunday christening is considered lucky and the child will grow up devout.

A child should always be dressed in white at its christening. Red ribbons should be avoided.

Three aritcles are frequently given a child when it is taken to be christened: egg, salt and a coin. These will give it strength, happiness and wealth.

Baptism in a church is luckier than in private.

When a child gives a lusty yell during its christening, it is a sign that it will have strong lungs through life.

If two children, a male and a female, are baptised together, the male should have the preference or it will grow up to be effeminate.

BELIEFS CONCERNING CHILDREN

It is unlucky to measure a baby with a string or tape measure, as it may stop growing.

To step over a young child is unlucky and may stunt its growth.

To hand a child through an open window will stop the little one's growth.

Children that cry a lot are sure to be lucky. They will develop fine eyes and broad shoulders. This does not apply where the crying is caused by illness or pain.

Women in pregnancy often refuse to take an oath before an officer of the court as it is supposed to influence the unborn child.

It is supposed to be unlucky for a child to walk backward when going on an errand.

In Scotland, when a young baby is taken out for its first airing, the mother or nurse gives something to eat to the first person she meets. This ensures the baby's good luck. It is called "the bairn's piece."

When a child is taken from its mother and carried out of the bedroom for the first time, it is luckier to take it upstairs than down. If there is no upstairs, the same effect can be accomplished by mounting a short elevation, a platform, or the rung of a ladder.

When a baby is carried to church to be baptized, it should be carried by a woman who is known to have had good luck.

When a baby is carried into a neighbor's house for the first time, it should be carried there by the mother herself, in order to insure good luck.

First of all, however, the baby should be carried to church.

A creeping child will have better luck than one that does not creep.

When a very young baby smiles in its sleep, it is supposed to hold converse with the angels.

BELIEFS CONCERNING EGGS

Eggs have many mystic meanings, and in olden times were supposed to symbolize the world. The yoke represented our earth, the white was its atmosphere, and the shell was the firmament. It was believed that the universe had its origin in an egg, and that God brooded over it until it was hatched out. Milton says: "Dovelike satst brooding o'er the vast abyss."

According to an old theorist, the egg typified the Messiah, the seed that was to bring forth salvation. The Abyssinians portray the world as a great ostrich egg.

The Syrians used to speak of their ancestors as the progeny of eggs. The Hawaiians believe that their island was produced by the bursting of a huge egg which had been laid on the water by a bird.

The ancients often said, "Everything springs from the egg. It is Nature's cradle."

Egyptians worshipped Cneph, the architect of the world, who was represented with an egg coming out of his mouth.

The druids used eggs in their religious festivals and considered it the symbol of fecundity. Every druid wore an egg about his neck, encased in gold, as a symbol of his priestly authority.

The Jews use an egg in their Passover service as a symbol of Divine Power and help.

Eggs laid on Good Friday are revered in Catholic countries as bringing good luck, and are carefully kept all year as talismans. They are supposed to keep the house free from fire.

In Scotland an "eirack's" egg, that is, the first egg that is laid by a young hen, is gathered as the principal ingredient of Hallowe'en charm. At midnight the egg is broken so that the white issues out drop by drop. It is allowed to fall into a wine glass two-thirds full of water. The palm of the hand is placed over the rim of the glass which is turned bottom up, and the albumen settles down near the hand. It assumes vague, shadowy forms which foretell the occupation the person will best thrive in. Thus, if it looks like a ship, the man should become a sailor.

Another custom in connection with an "eirack's" egg, is to take the white in one's mouth and go out into the night without swallowing a drop. If one hears the name of a man or woman called out aloud, it foretells the name of the future wife or husband.

Among other curious Hallowe'en customs is the following: Take a hard-boiled egg, remove some of the yoke, and fill it up with salt. Then eat the egg, salt and shell. Do not drink a drop of water till morning. If you dream of a person of the opposite sex, it means a marriage, but if the person you dream of seems to offer you a glass of water, it means that you will be jilted.

Birds' eggs have been believed to have many mysterious qualities. The eggs of an owl put into the cup of a drunkard will cause a loathing of liquor.

A stork's egg was also considered as a cure of the habit of drinking.

Persons afflicted with ague are instructed to visit the nearest crossroads five times in succession and there bury a new-laid egg. Their disease will leave them by morning and never return.

Strict silence must be maintained during the whole operation, as to speak to any one would prevent its success.

For the plague, eggs were often prescribed. They were usually filled with drugs.

It is believed in England's rural districts that if one brings primroses into a house, the number must be at least thirteen, as the hens about the place will only hatch so many eggs during the season as there are primroses.

When flowers blossom early and are numerous, it is believed that hens lay more than in other seasons.

When owners of horses eat eggs, it is said that they should eat an even number, otherwise some mischief will befall their horses. Grooms are not allowed to eat eggs, and jockeys must wash their hands after eating them.

Farmers' wives usually set their hens on an odd number of eggs, for to set them on an even number often results in a failure to hatch out a brood.

In Derbyshire the number of eggs put under a hen must be either eleven or thirteen. If twelve hens are set, the brood will not hatch out, or will come to grief afterward.

In setting a litter of eggs under a hen it is lucky to swing a lighted candle over the nest as a charm to prevent hawks or other animals from destroying the eggs or the young chicks.

In some Catholic countries, the tenth egg laid by a fowl is supposed to be bigger than the rest, and is usually offered to the priest.

Breaking egg shells over a child is supposed to keep him safe from witchcraft.

The goose that lays a golden egg is a popular myth in many countries. To receive such a valuable gift, it is necessary to invoke the name and help of the devil.

In some sections, it is considered unlucky to let eggs go out of the house after sunset. It is also considered unlucky to gather eggs after dark. All eggs should be gathered in the forenoon. It is unlucky to gather eggs on Sunday or to set a hen on the Sabbath.

Duck's eggs, brought into the house after sunset will never hatch.

Egg shells should not be burned, or the hens will cease to lay.

Eggs brought into the house or barn over running water, will not hatch.

When a child visits a house for the first time,

it is lucky to give him an egg that was laid that morning. It will give the child a "start in life" that will bring success.

To dream of an egg is lucky and means that a fortune is at hand.

Strings of blown egg shells hung up in a dwelling are unlucky, but if hung up in an outhouse, bring good luck.

Bats were supposed to come from eggs that had been hatched out by toads.

In Java the bride, as a sign of submission, kneels before her master, then treads upon an egg and washes his feet with the yoke.

The offering of an omelette to a newly married man by his mother-in-law, as a sign of devotion, is an old custom in Russia..

CHARMS AND AMULETS

The word "amulet" comes from the Arab, "Hamala," which means to carry about. It is a charm or object usually hung about the neck or on the wrist to ward off sickness and evil. A charm is similar in its effect.

People are spoken of as having a charmed life, which means that they seem to be immune to accidents or illness. Many wear charms to insure this result.

Some charms are engraved with peculiar figures called "talismans," which are supposed to have the power to prevent loss or illness. They are often engraved on some seal or precious stone, and worn on the finger or on a chain about the neck.

The practice of wearing charms or amulets is very ancient, and many of the objects found in Egyptian tombs are amulets, intended to serve the spirits of the dead. Many charms have obtained historic importance, as for instance the famous Spanish opal in the British museum.

The czar was supposed to be fond of an ancient ring in which is embedded a piece of the true cross. It was supposed to shield its wearer from death and danger, although it hardly helped him to keep his throne. He attached such importance to it, that on one occasion he started out on a journey without it, when suddenly discovering his loss, he delayed the trip eight hours till a messenger went and got it.

Oriental wrestlers will not go into the prize ring without wearing a charm about their necks.

Modern folks for the most part wear some sort

of amulet, or carry a charm in their pockets, but they do it secretly. They may not actually believe in its efficacy but want to get the benefit of it in case it should have some hidden virtue.

Horseshoe-shaped pins, or charms, are considered very lucky, so is four-leaved clover. Wishbones, too, have come into favor in recent years as they are supposed to have the power of making one's wishes come true.

Little pigs are popular as charms, as they are supposed to bring good luck. In fact, the Germans say, *"Ich habe Schwein,"* when they want to signify that they are lucky.

Lucky pennies or other coins are to be found in many pockets. They drive away evil influences in business operations and bring luck in money matters. They must be turned over in one's pocket at the time of the transaction.

Horse chestnuts or a small potato are considered efficacious charms against rheumatism. They must be carried in the pocket where they soon become hard and absorb all tendency to disease.

The relics of the saints, such as particles of bones, bits of hair, etc., or splinters from the cross, have been revered in all Christian lands for their miracle-working powers. Many churches

62 SIGNS, OMENS AND SUPERSTITIONS

have been erected and many shrines dedicated to house some such precious relic.

At St. Ann de Beau Pre Church near Quebec, and at St. Ann Church in New York, wonders are performed daily and many cripples healed through touching the particle of bone of the Virgin's mother.

A charm with the figure of a fish or the word "Ichthus," formed by the Greek initials of the name of Jesus, is worn by the Greek Christians and brings success.

Coins and bits of metal stamped with a cross are worn about the neck in many lands as a guarantee of good luck. They are also looked upon as a cure of epilepsy.

Rings with religious signs and symbols are often used to cure disease or insure success of the crops.

In the Orient, jade or ornaments from this stone are used as charms against disease or disaster. They usually have some symbolic figures carved upon them.

Jet was and in some countries is still supposed to exert a remarkable power over the brain and nerves, and is therefore much prized for jewelry

SIGNS, OMENS AND SUPERSTITIONS

and charms. It was supposed in olden days to drive away devils and serpents.

Amber is a favorite substance for charms in countries adjoining the Mediterranean. It is supposed to keep off infectious disease, epilepsy and other evils. It is frequently made into necklaces for babies.

Many other stones, gems or natural substances are used the world over for their supposed curative powers, and huge volumes have been written concerning them.

Adder stones are supposed to be efficacious against disease of cattle.

Carrying a human molar tooth as a charm is often considered a remedy for toothache.

Amulets to insure victory are frequent, and many a soldier goes into battle in the firm belief that the amulet he wears about his neck or on his arm will see him safely through. Bibles carried about the person are supposed to be the most efficacious of these, and in point of fact many a bullet has been stopped by a Bible placed near the heart.

During a plague in England red tape was in great demand to ward off the evil. It was cut into half-yard lengths and worn about the neck until all danger was past.

Amber and coral necklaces are often placed on children to give them relief from teething. Rings and nipples of these substances are provided for similar purposes.

A charm consisting of laurel leaves is often worn as a protection against lightning.

Scapulars, pieces of brown cloth in which are stitched certain verses from the New Testament, are worn to a great extent by Catholics as a preventive against perils of flood and sickness.

MASCOTS

The word "mascot" is of French origin and designates anything from a piece of string to a human being that is supposed to influence the Fates for the benefit of the possessor. A comic opera has been built around the idea, in which a king has very bad luck, until a pretty girl is sent to him as a mascot, when his fortune begins.

Ships often take a mascot on board before they sail. This is usually a dog, monkey or goat, and insures a pleasant voyage.

Regiments of soldiers usually adopt a mascot, an animal that accompanies them on their marches.

Baseball and football teams take a mascot with them to insure victory.

Mascots frequently take the shape of a horseshoe, charm, four-leaf clover or amulet to be worn on the person.

The popularity of mascots and in fact all objects that are supposed to bring luck is best explained by the fact that they suggest luck, and the owner acts on the suggestion. A person believing that some object is going to bring him fortune, will act with greater faith and assurance, thus bringing about the condition which he desires.

In regard to charms the decorative feature appeals to many; fear and imagination come next in their influence on the mind.

Regarding human mascots, their influence is supposed to be hereditary.

HORSESHOE LORE

The origin of a belief in the horseshoe as an emblem of good luck can be traced to the ancient days of phallic worship. The peculiar shape of the shoe became the emblem of sex and of productivity. It is a very old belief, therefore, that a horseshoe will have an influence for good.

The Moors believed in the horseshoe to such an extent that their architecture reflects it. Their mosque and temples all show an arch formation that had its origin in the form of a shoe, and they believed that this would insure stability.

The druids also believed in its efficacy, and many of their religious places, like Stonehenge in England, have the semi-circular form of a horseshoe.

An old Roman general ascribed his defeat to the loss of a horseshoe. Benjamin Franklin paraphrased this by writing: "Through the loss of a nail a shoe was lost, through the loss of a shoe a horse was lost, through the loss of a horse a battle was lost."

To find a horseshoe is considered lucky. It should be hung over the door of the house or barn. It will ensure a good harvest if suspended over the barn.

A horseshoe should be hung with the open ends upwards, so that it will "hold luck." If hung the other way, it will "spill luck."

When going on a long voyage, it will bring luck to carry a horseshoe in your baggage.

A scarfpin or watch charm in the shape of a horseshoe is lucky.

The wishbone, or collar bone of a chicken, is considered lucky on account of its resemblance in shape to a horseshoe. Two people, each pulling at one end, can determine who will get married first. The longer piece is the lucky one.

A horseshoe should have seven holes for nails, three on one side and four on the other side of the center heel. This will ensure double luck, as seven is a number of good fortune.

Rings made of horseshoe nails are sovereign remedies against bad luck, disease and trouble.

PIN SUPERSTITIONS

To pick up a pin is lucky; let it lie, is bad luck.

If a pin lies with its head toward you it is a good sign, but beware of trouble if the point is towards you.

To prick yourself with a pin on starting on a trip is a bad omen.

It will break friendship to present any one with a pin, such as a scarfpin or the like. Such a gift should be bought. A cent or article of minor importance must be given in exchange.

CHAPTER VII
THE INFLUENCES OF MYTHICAL BEINGS

The belief in fairies and other supernatural beings is universal, not only among children but among grown people as well, and many a quaint and interesting legend has been spun about these fascinating individuals. Fairy lore comprises the greater part of our books for young people, and without fairy tales the lives of children would be barren indeed. So, also, have many superstitions grown up about fairies, and they are believed in by folks that are intelligent as well as by those that are ignorant.

Fairies are supposed to be supernatural beings, human in form but very often diminutive, with superior powers for good or evil. They have the power of invisibility, but can become visible when they wish. They are often invoked for aid, but are never worshipped as were the goddesses of the pagan world. They enter the habitations of mortals and spread their gifts. Sometimes they do mischief. It is well to keep in the good graces of fairies.

The Hindoos believe in a kind of fairy that they call "Acvins." These assist in bringing lovers together, give succor in trouble and bring wealth to the deserving.

Persians believe in Peris, delicate ethereal females, who while not immortal, live very long. To assist or otherwise get into the good graces of a Peri means good luck, but to offend one, brings bad luck.

The Arabian "Jinns" are fairies of a more austere kind. They are males who can do great damage if offended and whom it is therefore well to placate. They are supposed to have lived before Adam and were once a mighty race, but war and accident have slain many. Every time a star shoots across the sky it means the death of a jinn. They have the power to make themselves visible or invisible.

The Jews believed in Shedim, a species of fairy that was the offspring of Adam. These beings have wings, are similar to angels, eat, drink, make merry, and help any mortal who is kind to them.

The Greeks and Romans had their own conceptions of fairies. They called them dryads, naiads, fauns, satyrs, etc. They mingled with mortals and often intermarried with them. They brought luck or the reverse as they were favorably inclined. They rewarded any kindness and punished transgressions.

Fata Morgana is the Italian conception of a fairy, the personification of Fortune. Happy the person who wins her favor.

In France, fairies have different names and characteristics. There are *"follets"* who are always invisible but whose voices are often heard. They are mischievous and pelt the peasants with stones. They often enter a house and throw about the utensils and create disorder from a sense of humor that is often hard to understand. Where a man is in their good graces, however, they do good and reward virtues. It is considered lucky to come across their tracks or circles in the grass.

The French also believe in *fees, lutins* and goblins. These dance in circles, or fairy rings by night, haunt solitary springs and grottoes, ride horses and tie up the horses manes to form stirrups. They preside at births, bring luck to babies in whom they take an interest, give presents, help along the lovelorn, and do other stunts. They often take a child out of its cradle and leave one of their own brood in its place. This is called a "changeling," and while such child is apt to be beautiful, its propensities are for evil.

Scandinavians believe in elves, playful, malicious beings that are up to all sorts of mischief. They delight in perplexing people, tie the hair of sleeping children into knots, steal away articles, and cause no end of trouble. It is well to propitiate them by kindness, and by leaving something for them to eat in the grottoes where they are supposed to dwell.

Teutonic races have their fairies, trolls, gnomes, dwarfs, who do all manner of mischief. Many are the strange tales told about them, and many are the rites and ceremonies resorted to by the peasantry to get into their good graces.

The Irish are great believers in fairies, and their literature is filled with tales of their deeds. Their superstitions concerning them would fill a good-sized book. They dress in green, are very pretty and benevolent, help the peasants, bring lovers together, avoid law suits, do good by stealth, etc.

Brownies and kelpies are the Scotch brand of fairies. They often appear in the form of cattle or horses, and when people ride on them, they throw them off and play other tricks. They are as mischievous as children, but do nothing particularly praiseworthy.

English have their fairies, hobgoblins, Robin Goodfellow, Puck, and other well-known characters. Shakespeare assembled them in one large clan, with Oberon as their king and Titania as their queen. They are a well-behaved crew, full of mischief but with good traits as well.

Some of the more prominent superstitions concerning fairies are the following:

A mole or defect on a person is supposed to be caused by a fairy nipping him before birth.

A matted lock near the neck of a sleeping child is called an elflock and is the deed of a mischievous fairy.

To throw away a peach stone out of a window is dangerous as it might strike a fairy and kill it. This would bring bad luck for seven years.

Four-leaved clover usually marks the spot where fairies congregate and bring good luck.

Round circles often found in the grass indicate the place where fairies dance. To sit in such a circle with one of the opposite sex, is sure to bring about a marriage.

When a child is lucky it is a sure proof that

a fairy godmother stood at its cradle at its birth.

Fossil Echini turned up by the plow, are called fairy loaves. If you keep a fairy loaf in the house, you will never want for bread.

If one comes across a "fairy ring," it is luckier to walk around it than across it.

If you run around a "fairy ring" nine times, you can hear the sounds of merriment caused by the fairies dancing under ground.

Fairies reward servants for cleanliness by putting a coin in their shoes.

A fairy entering a dairy spoils the cream.

In many sections of England a prayerbook is put under a child's pillow to keep away fairies and pixies.

Lumbago, epilepsy and fits are supposed to be caused by a shot from a malignant fairy.

A knot hole in a deal door is bad as it will let fairies in. It must be plugged up at once.

WITCHES

The belief in witches is very old. At times in the history of mankind it has become epidemic and done untold damage. In the seventeenth century thousands of old women were burned at the stake for their supposed intercourse with the devil. Doctors and judges as well as ignorant people believed in this nonsense. The witch was supposed to be a woman who had sold her soul to the devil, and frequented the Devil's Sabbath, riding thither on a broomstick. In rural districts the belief still prevails to some extent.

When horses break out in a sweat in the stable, it is believed that a witch has been riding them.

When a horse's mane is tangled, a witch is supposed to have tied the knot to use as a stirrup.

Shoulder bones of sheep are called "hagbones" because witches are believed to ride on them.

Eggshells must be broken and not left to lie about the house, or they may be used by witches as boats.

When sick people go into a decline, they are said to be "overlooked" or bewitched, and there is little hope for their recovery.

A white witch is one who has the power to remove the spell of a bad witch. There are various incantations by which this is done.

To prevent a witch from injuring a person,

SIGNS, OMENS AND SUPERSTITIONS

he must make an image of wax of the witch and stick it full of pins. This will cause the witch to become impotent and die.

Wearing the left stocking inside out, horseshoes, spittle, hagstones, etc., are good antidotes to a witch's power. The sign of the cross also prevents their evil.

CHAPTER VIII
SIGNS CONNECTED WITH THE BODY.
SNEEZING

The custom of muttering a prayer or a pious wish after sneezing is as old as history. It was accounted very ancient in the time of Aristotle, who in his "Problems" endeavored to account for it, but knew nothing of its origin. According to him the ancients believed that the head was the seat of the soul and that sneezing in some way affected the spirit. Hence the necessity of uttering an invocation to preserve the soul from harm.

The Greeks and Romans had a number of formulas for sneezing, such as, "Long may you live!" "May you enjoy good health!" "Jupiter preserve you!"

Sneezing was often considered a lucky omen among the ancients. Their history is full of events of importance which were ushered in by a sneeze. The "Odyssey" tells of the "lucky sneeze of Telemachus." History tells of the soldiers' sneezing in adoration of a god that rose before them in the ranks, an event which Xenophon regarded as a favorable omen.

Aristotle considered a sneeze as divine, but a cough as vulgar. Petronius mentions the custom of saying, *"Salve"* (hail), when a soldier sneezed. Tiberius Cæsar never neglected to observe this formula.

When a Hindoo sneezes, bystanders say, "Live!" and he replies, "With you!" The Zulus believe that an angry spirit enters the body and that a sneeze is an effort of nature to expel it.

Aristotle believed that sneezing from noon till midnight was a good omen, but from midnight till the next noon was a sign of bad luck.

All nations have some formula for sneezing. The Germans say, *"Zur Gesundheit!"* The English say, "God bless you!" The French say, *"A vos souhaits."*

If some one sneezes after you have made a statement, it places the seal of truth upon it and the statement may not be doubted.

According to mythology Prometheus made an artificial man, and the first sign of life he gave was to sneeze. It was through the nostril that life entered into his body.

In the time of Pope St. Gregory the Great,

there was an epidemic of sneezing, and many of the afflicted died. The pope thereupon declared that a certain prayer should be uttered every time a person sneezed, to avert the calamity.

To sneeze three times in rapid succession is considered a good omen.

Physiologically considered in the light of modern science, sneezing is bad, as it spreads the germs of many diseases by spraying them into the air. One should always sneeze into a handkerchief.

SPITTING

In ancient times spitting was considered as having the virtue of averting witchcraft, and even in our time many superstitions cling to the habit.

Spit was considered as a charm against all kinds of fascination. Theocritus says:

"Thrice on my breast I spit to guard me safe from fascinating charms."

Superstitious nurses will spit on their children to keep them from harm.

Alluding to this custom an ancient writer says: "His lips are wet with lustral spittle, thus

They think to make the gods propitious."

Bruisers and boxers before attacking their adversary, spit on their hands to insure success.

Boys, when making a pledge or asserting a thing to be "honor bright," often spit on the ground to give emphasis to their good faith.

Coal miners in England when they form a union for any purpose, sit in a circle and spit on a stone, by way of cementing their friendship and loyalty.

Devout people often spit at the mention of the name of his satanic majesty, in an effort to keep away evil influences.

Mohammedans are said to spit at the mention of the name of Jesus.

To spit on one's hands before undertaking a piece of manual work insures a successful result.

Spitting three times into their bosoms, was considered by the Greeks as preventive of danger when in the presence of a madman or an epileptic.

When a man hit another and felt remorse for the blow, he spit into the hollow of his hand, and thus freed the other from pain. This was a superstition of the Middle Ages.

Spitting to avert evil influences is still resorted

to among country folks, and in some countries is almost considered a religious act.

In Ireland it is considered unlucky to praise a horse or other animal unless you spit on him and say, "God save him," or other similar prayer. If after three days, any bad luck befalls the animal, it is necessary to find the person who praised him so that he may whisper the Lord's Prayer into the animal's right ear.

Hucksters, peddlers, and other tradespeople, have a habit of spitting for good luck when making a sale. The first money they receive in the morning is spat upon to insure good luck for the day.

It is customary in some parts when a rainbow appears to make a cross on the ground and spit on each of the four corners.

MOLES, TEETH, WARTS, ETC.

Moles may denote good or bad fortune according to where they are found.

On the throat they are lucky; on the lower jaw, especially of a woman, they denote the opposite. On the back of the neck they are said to predict a hanging.

Red or black moles are considered unlucky,

but brown ones are lucky. If raised like a wart they foretell luck.

A mole on the forehead brings good fortune, so also one on the chin. As a rule moles denote coming wealth.

The hairs growing out of moles are considered harbingers of fortune and in some countries are carefully guarded and cultivated. In Latin countries one can see men go about with long hairs growing out of moles on their faces. They are careful never to shave them.

When a child loses a tooth it will hasten the growth of the new tooth, if the old is thrown into the fire.

When a tooth is pulled it should be thrown into the fire. In Switzerland it is carefully wrapped in paper with a pinch of salt and burned.

To cure a toothache, the name of St. Apollonia is invoked in Latin countries. She suffered martyrdom by having her teeth pulled out, and has since been the patron saint of those who suffer from similar pangs.

To dream of losing a tooth, foretells the death of a friend.

If a baby's tooth first appars in the upper jaw, it is a sign that the child will die in infancy.

If the teeth are very irregular it is a sign of bad luck.

If there is a gap between the two upper middle teeth large enough to pass a coin through, it foretells wealth.

The Greeks believed that it was unlucky to count one's warts as they would increase in number.

To charm away a wart, buy it from the possessor for a pin, and it will disappear within a week.

Another way to charm away a wart is to rub it with half an apple. Tie the two halves together with a thread, and bury it at the foot of a tree. Within a week the wart will have disappeared.

Spots in the nails foretell riches. If many, the person showing them will gain a fortune. White specks often foretell happenings without wealth. On the thumb-nail, they indicate honors.

YAWNING

Among many peoples, yawning is considered a sign of possession or obsession by an evil spirit.

When the Hindoo yawns, he snaps his thumb

and finger and repeats the name of one of his deities. To neglect this brings misfortune.

When a Moslem yawns he puts the back of his left hand to his mouth and says, "I seek refuge with Allah from Satan."

There is an old belief that when one yawns the devil may leap into the open mouth; hence the necessity of holding a hand over the mouth.

To yawn in the midst of saying one's prayers, is a bad omen. It is better to say the prayer from the beginning again.

TINGLING AND ITCHING

It is a common superstition that when one's ears tingle some one is talking about him.

Shakespeare says in "Much Ado About Nothing," "What fire is in mine ears?" Beatrice deduces from this that a friend is talking about her.

Even the old Roman historian, Pliny, says: "It is an opinion generally received that when our ears do glow and tingle, there be some that in our absence do talk of us."

The tingling of the right ear is taken to mean that good is spoken, while, that of the left ear is a token of the fact that evil is spoken.

Herrick writes:
> "My ear tingles, some there be
> That are snarling now at me."

The itching of the palm is considered an indication that the person will get some unexpected money. If continued for any length of time, a fortune will come to him.

The itching of the thumb or nose denotes a visitor, sometimes an unwelcome intruder.

One of the witches in "Macbeth" says:
> "By the pricking of my thumbs,
> Something wicked this way comes."

STUMBLING AND FALLING

Falling has always been associated with the idea of evil, and its effects can only be averted by a quick-witted remark or a muttered invocation.

When Cæsar landed at Adrumetum in Africa, it is related that he tripped and fell upon his face. This was considered as an ill omen by his soldiers, but with great presence of mind he exclaimed: "Thus do I take possession of thee, O Africa." Thus he changed a sign of bad to one of good fortune.

When William the Conqueror landed in England, he fell prone upon the ground. A great cry of despair went up from his army, but he raised himself smilingly and said: "I have seized the country with both my hands."

To fall while going upstairs is a sure sign that the victim will not marry within a year.

The falling of a picture from the wall is universally regarded as a bad omen and frequently foretells the death of the original of the picture in the case of a portrait.

It is related that a well-known English archbishop on entering his study one day, found his portrait lying on the floor, the cord that held it on the hook, having snapped. The sight so unnerved the prelate that he became ill, and died shortly after.

The Duke of Buckingham had a similar misadventure. On entering the council chamber, he found his portrait lying at full length on the floor. He died soon after.

A fall from a horse, besides being very inconvenient and often painful, is supposed to bring evil consequences. If two persons part on horseback, and one of them falls off his mount, the two will never meet again.

The fall of a window blind is accounted unlucky, but the evil can be averted by at once replacing it in its sockets.

The fall of a knife or fork to the floor is usually considered a good omen and foretells a visit from a friend; a female in the case of a knife, or a male in the case of a fork.

To fall downstairs is a very bad sign and signifies loss of health or money.

To stumble in the morning on coming downstairs is a sign of ill luck during the day.

A horse stumbling on the highway brings bad luck to his owner.

Stumbling at a grave is considered a bad omen. Shakespeare says:

"How oft to-night

"Have my old feet stumbled at graves!"

"For many men that stumble at the threshold

"Are well foretold that danger lurks within."

If you stumble over a stick or stone, turn back and kick it out of the way to avert trouble.

CUTTING NAILS AND HAIR

The paring of nails has given rise to some strange beliefs. So also has the cutting of hair.

This is natural, as the clipping away of one's body is in itself uncanny and apt to give rise to superstitious conjectures.

Sailors believe that to cut the nails or hair during a calm will provoke contrary winds. They, therefore, only cut them in a storm.

The ancients declared that nails and hair should not be pared or cut when in the presence of the gods, but in the secrecy of one's home.

Among the Arabians it is considered lucky to cut the nails and hair on Friday.

In some countries it is considered unlucky to cut a child's nails till it is a year old. They have to be bitten off.

In Scotland it is believed that if a child's nails are cut before it is a year old, it will grow up to be a thief. In other lands, it is thought the child will stammer.

The Jews burn their nail parings with a piece of wood, as a species of offering to insure good luck.

PERSONAL APPEARANCE

When a woman's eyebrows meet across her nose, it is a good sign. She will be happy whether she marries or not.

A woman whose hair grows down over her forehead in the shape of a peak, will never marry.

CLOTHES SUPERSTITIONS

On rising in the morning, great care must be given to the way one dresses, as accidents often foretell trouble during the day.

Augustus Cæsar put on his left sandal awry and nearly lost his life in a mutiny. A well-known writer says:

"Augustus by an oversight
Put on his left shoe before his right;
Had like to have been slain that day
By soldiers mutinying for pay."

To put your shirt inside out is a good omen, providing you discover it in time and change it. If left on all day, beware of accidents.

To button your vest so that the buttons and holes come out uneven is a good sign.

It is well to put on the stocking of your right foot first and the shoe of your left foot.

To tear off a button while dressing is a bad sign. It should be remedied at once before going out of the house.

A hole in one's stocking is a good sign on the first day, but brings bad luck on the second.

To put the right shoe on the left foot or the reverse, is a sign of coming trouble.

To rip a garment the first time you put it on, is a bad sign.

To rend one's garments was in former days considered a symbol of mourning.

If you meet a person wearing new clothes, pinch him for good luck.

A proverbial saying when meeting a person with new clothes, is, "May you have health to wear it, strength to tear it, and money to buy another."

Coin given to a person wearing a new suit will bring him good fortune as long as the clothes last.

To put on a suit for the first time on Monday signifies that it will soon tear. You will have bad luck in wearing it.

Tuesday—Beware lest the suit catch fire. Keep out of speculation.

Wednesday—Things will go well with you. Your speculations will succeed.

Thursday—You will always appear neat and well dressed. You will make a good impression and get what you are after.

Friday—Not a good day to put on new attire.

You will be successful only as long as the clothes remain fresh.

Saturday—Beware of catching cold. There is an element of bad luck in a new suit on this day.

Sunday—Happiness and good luck will follow him who puts on a new suit on the Sabbath.

ON ARISING

To get out of bed with the left foot is considered a forecast of bad luck. When a person is cross or irritable, we often say, "He got out of bed with the wrong foot."

To put your foot on a soft carpet or rug, on arising, foretells a successful day.

To stumble on getting up, is bad. You should go back to bed and try it again.

To say "Good luck" on arising, will insure success during the day.

It is considered unlucky to sing before breakfast. You may cry before supper.

It is unlucky to relate a bad dream before breakfast. It may come true.

To find a coin early in the morning is a sign for you to beware lest you lose money before the day is spent.

SQUINTING, CRIPPLED AND HUNCHBACK PERSONS

To meet a squinting or cross-eyed person on going out in the morning is a sign of trouble. It is well to go back a block or two and start over.

To walk with a cross-eyed person is sure to bring bad luck.

To touch a hunchback's hump brings good luck. Gamblers, especially, often resort to this method to change their luck from bad to good.

To have a hunchback about the premises brings good fortune. In former years kings used to have a court fool who was usually a hunchback, not only to make merriment for them, but to insure good fortune.

To shake hands with a left-handed person is often regarded as unlucky.

To touch a blind man's garment or brush past him is a sign of ill fortune. To help a blind man on his way, is an omen of good luck.

To be baptized by a left-handed priest is considered unlucky.

To meet a priest the first thing in the morning is a bad omen. This may be averted by throwing a pin at him.

To have a cripple tread on your toes is a very bad omen.

To meet a beggar as you leave your house in the morning, is a bad sign, and you should at once return and start over.

To give a coin to a cripple insures good luck.

DEATH AND CORPSES

Feathers or a bird in the room of a sick person are supposed to delay death. This idea is often resorted to where it is advisable to delay the last breadth till some absent friend arrives.

At the moment of death the doors and windows are often opened to allow the spirit free egress.

Looking-glasses and pictures are covered as long as the corpse is in the house, to prevent the spirit from seeing its reflection.

In Scotland a piece of iron is thrust into all eatables right after a death, to prevent the attraction of other spirits.

A plate of salt is put upon the breast of a new corpse in Wales to purge out all the sins of the defunct.

Candles are lit at the head of the corpse, to ward off evil spirits.

A watch is usually kept by the side of the body

SIGNS, OMENS AND SUPERSTITIONS

until the funeral, to ward off evil spirits and also rats.

Tolling of the bell is usual in most countries. After some minutes of tolling there is a pause, and three times three tolls for a male and twice three for a female, is the rule.

Where bees are kept it is customary to tell the bees that their owner is dead and that they must remain and work for the new owner.

In Ireland a wake is the rule. Friends of the departed meet and discuss the good points and foibles of the dead. Refreshments are served.

THE EVIL EYE

The fear of the evil eye is very prevalent among the Latin races, and even in this country there is a belief that certain persons possess the *"mal occhio"* and can bewitch by merely looking with hatred or envy upon another. Many charms and amulets have and are still being worn to counteract any bad effects.

A cross of jet is frequently used as an amulet against the evil eye. It is believed that it will split if looked upon by a person having evil intentions.

The following are a few of the many substances used for averting the evil from this source. Skin from a hyenna's forehead, madwort hung up in the home; Catochites, a species of stone, worn in a ring or about the neck; spitting on the right shoe before putting it on; a necklace of jacinth, etc.

Sweeping a child's face with the bough of a pine tree, is considered a very successful preventive; so is hanging up the key of the house over a child's cradle.

Other means of preventing the blasting effects of the evil eye are: Laying turf, dug from a grave, upon the cradle of a child; laying crumbs on the cradle; giving the child a piece of coral that was dipped in the font in which the child was baptized.

Hindoos decorate their children with a profusion of jewels to antagonize the evil eye. Mohammedans suspend articles from the ceiling over the cradle for the same purpose.

In Roumania a child or grown person decorated with red ribbons is supposed to be impervious to this terrible influence, and hence most people wear something scarlet about their bodies, and even the oxen in the field have something red tied about their horns.

CHAPTER IX
HOUSEHOLD BELIEFS

If the keys of a careful housewife get rusty in spite of her care, it means that some one is saving money for her.

A hot cinder jumping out of the grate signifies the coming of good fortune.

If meat shrinks while being boiled in a pot, it is a bad sign, but if it swells, it means that prosperity is in store.

The first cake taken out of an oven should be broken, not cut; otherwise all the rest of the cakes baked that day will be soggy.

Do not sweep the dust out of the front door. It indicates that your good luck will be swept out with it.

If a leaf of soot hangs in the grate, it announces the coming of a guest.

If a rooster stands upon the threshold of your house and crows, a stranger may be expected.

If you neglect to close down the lid of your teapot, a guest will come and have tea with you.

If your tea-kettle sings, it is a sign of contentment in the home.

In sweeping, beware not to sweep the dirt over a girl's feet, as it will prevent her from marrying that year.

If you wash your hands and face in a bowl of water that has been used by some one else, it foretells a quarrel with that other person.

Trousers made on Friday are unlucky and will soon tear.

To break up your bread into crumbs at the table is an omen of coming poverty.

To drop a coarse comb foretells a visit by a man,—a fine-tooth-comb means a visit from a woman.

To throw away a piece of bread is an indication of carelessness and brings bad luck.

LOOKING-GLASS OMENS

Mirrors have always been regarded as divine instruments and used as objects of divination, hence a certain amount of superstition attaches to them. It is wonderful, indeed, that by nature's law of reflection, one can see the image of that which is outside of the glass, and it has been considered unlucky to destroy in any way that power to reflect.

To break a looking-glass is considered unlucky,

and the person breaking one will have bad fortune for seven years.

If the looking-glass is willfully broken and thrown away, it has no effect upon one's fortune.

In Catholic countries a person accidentally breaking a mirror, crosses himself and says: "May the Saints avert ill fortune." The curse is thereby lifted.

In the days of ancient Greece, divination was performed by means of water and a looking-glass. This was called catoptromancy. The mirror was dipped into the water and a sick person was asked to look into the glass. If his image appeared distorted, he was likely to die; if clear, he would live.

Looking-glasses are often used by fortune tellers in a way similar to crystal globes. They can tell from the nature of the images they perceive what will be the future of the inquirer.

To break the glass over a friend's portrait is a bad sign. It often betokens the death of the person who is the original of the picture.

It is considered ill luck to see your face in a mirror by candlelight.

SPILLING OF SALT

Salt has usually been considered in the light

of a sacrificial element. Greeks and Romans mixed it with their cakes that were offered up on the altars of their deities. It was a necessary part of the sacrifice. Hence any accident to the salt on a table was considered unlucky.

Among pagans salt was regarded as having redemptive power and was used when doing any important business as a preventive of ill luck. It was thrown on the ground with an invocation that was supposed to ward off unfriendly spirits.

Among the Jews, it is still a mark of hospitality to break bread with a stranger, and the bread is first dipped into salt. "Sharing one's salt with a stranger," has become synonymous with hospitality.

Salt has been regarded as the symbol of friendship, therefore the overturning of a salt-cellar is looked upon as the breaking of friendship.

To spill salt at table is considered unlucky. To change the spell, however, it is only necessary to take a pinch of the salt and throw it over the left shoulder.

In Da Vinci's picture of the Last Supper, Judas Iscariot is represented as overturning the salt. It is evident from this that the spilling of salt was considered a bad omen in the epoch when this picture was painted.

In some Eastern countries, the spilling of flour is viewed with the same feeling of awe as in the case of salt.

To put too much salt into the food when cooking, is supposed to be proof that the cook is in love.

KNIFE SUPERSTITIONS

It is considered unlucky to accept a knife from a friend without giving something in return. You therefore buy the knife and avert the "cutting of friendship."

A penny is usually offered in exchange for a knife, but among some believers, a pin is all that is necessary.

To drop a knife on the floor, means the coming of a visitor.

Knife and fork should never be crossed at the table, as this would presage bad luck. They should be laid side by side.

To cross knives is to invite a cross or misfortune. The origin of this belief probably lay in the disinclination to make the sign of the cross sacreligiously.

To leave a penknife open after you are through with it is a sign of danger and is unlucky.

To drop a knife accidentally so that the point penetrates into the ground and it stands upright is a sign of coming success.

To place an open knife near a sleeping child is considered a good omen.

CANDLE SUPERSTITIONS

Candles have always had a peculiarly religious character, and have from time immemorial been used in the service of churches and for sacred rites. Many queer superstitions attach to them.

In Catholic countries it is customary to bring candles to church in honor of one's favorite saint or of the Madonna. The size of the candle and its decoration gave evidence of the donor's religious enthusiasm.

Many of the saints had their own peculiar preferences as to the color of the candles.

A birthday cake should have as many candles on it as there are years in the person's age. This will ensure another year of happiness.

When the wax of a candle forms a loop like a handle, it is called a "coffin handle," and portends bad luck.

The dripping of tallow or wax down the side of a candle, is called a "shroud" and foretells death to the person towards whom it is directed.

A spark in the wick is called a "letter" and foretells the arrival of good news.

A knot in the wick, burning with a red glow, indicates the visit of a stranger.

A wick charred but remaining over the flame is a sign of good luck.

To kill a moth hovering about a candle is a harbinger of good luck.

CONCERNING LADDERS

To walk under a ladder when it is leaning against a wall, is a sign of bad luck.

To pass under a ladder that is hung horizontally does not influence your luck for good or evil.

To climb a ladder with an odd number of rungs is a good sign and leads to success.

To be on a ladder with a pretty girl is a good sign and foretells matrimony.

To fall from a ladder is an omen of ill luck and foretells a loss of money.

CHAPTER X

DIVINATION

THE MYSTERY OF NUMBERS

That there is virtue in numbers and that every person is under the influence of certain numbers was taught as far back as the days of Pythagoras, and a vast collection of books have been written concerning this phase of superstition.

Any clairvoyant to whom you may go to have fortune will ask you on what day of the month your fortune told will ask you on what day of the month you were born and in what year. From this she will tell you whether to expect good or evil fortune in the coming year. The basis for these calculations has been handed down from very ancient times.

According to astrologers, every letter in one's name corresponds to a number, so that if you understand how to calculate the numerical value of your name you can foretell your future.

The planets have numbers, and the influence they exert on you depends in how far their numbers correspond with those in your name and dates of important events in your life.

In horse racing, the names of the horses, taken according to their numerical value, often predict the result of the race.

Every nation had its lucky and unlucky numbers that occur in their mythology and history. The Greeks believed in the sacredness of the number nine. They had nine muses, nine principal deities, nine oracles, etc.

The Romans believed in the mystic three, the Egyptians in twelve, etc.

The Jews revered the number seven, and its recurrence throughout the Bible is remarkable: Seven days of creation, seven lean years, seven fat years, seven stars, seven times bathing in the Jordan, seven years followed by a year of jubilee, etc. This number, according to Kabala was obtained by adding the letters of Man and God together.

Thirteen, as we know, has been regarded by Christians as a very unlucky number on account of the events following the Last Supper.

Divination by numbers is a favorite pastime and leads to some remarkable results. Many historical events have been prophesied by this method. Thus Napoleon III was born in 1808 and assumed the empire in 1852. Add 1-8-0-8 to 1852 and you have 1869, which foretold the end of the empire about that time.

The French Revolution occurred in 1789; add this date to the sum of its numbers and you have 1814, which foretells the end of Napoleon's reign.

The dates of other personalities can be worked out the same way and the result is often remarkably correct.

Kabala, or the occult science of the Jews of the Middle Ages, depended almost entirely upon the mystic powers of numbers.

Many problems in modern mathematics depend on the mystic number nine and both nine and seven are used by fortune tellers in divining the future.

LOTTERY NUMBERS AND USAGES

Lotteries are practically a thing of the past in America, but there was a time when they flourished and when everybody from the wage earner to the millionaire wagered his pile on some lucky number. In the South the fever raged particularly strong, and the Louisiana Lottery and the Dismal Swamp Lottery counted their victims by the million. Policy, too, was very prevalent, and is still being conducted secretly in many parts of the country. Both lottery and policy were similar in that a certain price was paid for a ticket or a paper with numbers. On stated occasions numbers were drawn out of a wheel and these were announced. The holder of the lucky number won an amount that differed according to the occasion.

A man's age, or that of his wife or children, was frequently taken as the number. Some men added the figures in the date, month, etc.

Dreams are considered particularly efficacious in playing policy. Most dream books give policy numbers coinciding with every possible dream, and these when played are supposed to make a winning.

Among the numbers often taken are the date of the year, or the date of an important event. The numbers on a freight car have been known to bring fortunate results.

In the case of a murder committed in a community, certain numbers are supposed to have a peculiar significance and bring luck.

In the South many negroes make a comfortable living by interpreting dreams, signs and omens and telling the proper numbers they signify for the playing of policy.

In buying several lottery tickets, it is not lucky to have them all follow each other consecutively. An interval should separate them.

Odd numbers are more apt to bring prizes than even numbers. Numbers ending in three, nine, twelve or seven are the most likely to strike luck.

A number given you by a cripple is sure to be successful, but that given by a cross-eyed man or woman is bound to lose.

PREDICTIONS OF WEALTH

To have lots of hair on your arms and fingers is a sign of coming wealth.

When you throw a lump of sugar into your coffee or tea, the number of bubbles that arise are an indication of your future wealth.

Many moles over your body indicate that you will be wealthy.

To be born with a caul indicates that you will have luck and amass wealth.

A birthmark in the middle of the back indicates a wealthy marriage.

To be born during an eclipse, denotes hardship and poverty.

DIVINATION BY LETTERS

The most celebrated arrangement of letters by which fortunes were told or cures effected was the ABRACADABRA. It is attributed to Serenus, a celebrated physician of the second century. It is often written so that reading from the apex like an inverted pyramid up to the right side, the same word will be spelled as at the top. Thus:

```
A B R A C A D A B R A
A B R A C A D A B R
A B R A C A D A B
A B R A C A D A
A B R A C A D
A B R A C A
A B R A C
A B R A
A B R
A B
A
```

The belief in the wonderful powers of this word are well-nigh universal. By writing it on a parchment and hanging it about the neck of a sick person, it would staunch blood, heal disorders, cure toothache, etc.

The Jews used a similar word, Abracalam,

to cure disorders. In the Middle Ages the word, Anamazaptas, if whispered into a man's ear, was supposed to cure epilepsy.

The word "Bedooh" inscribed on rings and charms or on helmets or sabres is supposed to bring good luck. It comes from an Arab word which means "he has walked well."

The word "Osy" was used as a charm against serpents, and caused them to lie still as the dead.

Pythagoras considered the letter Y a symbol of life, and used it in his divinations.

Anagrams are often used to tell fortunes and to decide the career of a person. Thus Eleanor Davies, a well-known English woman and the wife of a poet, became a prophetess because she found that the letters of her name could be transposed to read, "Reveal O Daniel."

In many countries, charms worn about the neck and engraved with mystic letters have the power to keep away evil and cure disease.

DIVINATION BY BOOKS

In ancient Greece, when people wanted counsel on important matters, they opened a scroll of Homer at random and noted the lines covered by the thumb. At the present time the Bible is the book usually employed for that purpose.

If in distress, open the Bible and put your index finger on the page at random. The text will tell you what to do. If the words have no apparent bearing on the question, you should consider it an unfavorable reply.

To decide Yes or No in any doubtful matter, open the Bible and note the first word on the left-hand page. If it has an even number of letters, the answer is No; if an odd number of letters, the answer is Yes.

If things have gone wrong with you, open the Bible and say:

"Mark and Matthew, Luke and John,
Counsel, that I may get on."

Then retire and inspiration will come in your sleep.

A singular mode of divination for girls who desire to know their fate is described in an old book, as follows:

"When you go to bed place under your pillow a prayer book opened at the part of the matrimonial service which begins, 'With this ring I thee wed,' etc." Place a key on it, a ring, a flower, a sprig of willow, a small heart-shaped cake, a crust of bread and a pack of playing cards. Wrap these up in a thin handkerchief and, on getting into bed, cross your thumbs and say:

'Luna, every woman's friend,
To me thy goodness condescend;
Let me this night in visions see
Emblems of my destiny.'"

On New Year's Day a Bible is laid on the table, in some parts of England, and each member of the family opens it at random and from the contents of the two open pages reads his destiny for the ensuing year.

The last chapter of the Book of Proverbs contains thirty-one verses, each of which is supposed to have reference to one day of a month. By consulting these for the day of the month on which you were born, you will have an indication as to which kind of occupation you will be most successful in. Thus, the twenty-fourth verse speaks of "fine linen," which indicates that the person born on that day will be successful as a manufacturer or seller of linen.

PRECIOUS STONES

Precious stones are supposed in all countries to have a special province in inducing fortunate

SIGNS, OMENS AND SUPERSTITIONS

or unlucky occurrences. The proper stone is chosen according to the month of one's birth, each month being governed by a different gem.

The following is the list of birth stones according to the generally accepted belief:

January,	Garnet
February,	Amethyst
March,	Bloodstone
April,	Diamond
May,	Emerald
June,	Agate
July,	Ruby
August,	Sardonyx
September,	Sapphire
October,	Opal
November,	Topaz
December,	Turquoise

In the dictionary of "Phrase and Fable," we find a different arrangement based on astrological lore. It is as follows:—

Sign of Zodiac	Month	Stone
Aries, the ram,	April	Amethyst
Taurus, the bull,	May	Agate
Gemini, the twins,	June	Beryl
Cancer, the crab,	July	Emerald

Sign of Zodiac	Month	Stone
Leo, the virgin,	August	Ruby
Libra, the balance,	September	Jasper
Scorpio, the scorpion,	October	Diamond
Sagittarius, archer,	November	Topaz
Capricorn, the goat,	January	Onyx
Aquarius, waterman,	February	Sapphire
Pisces, the fishes,	March	Chrysolite

A ring presented to a person with his or her birthstone is sure to bring good fortune.

One's birthstone in a charm or locket, worn about the neck, will bring luck in business or speculation.

COLOR SUPERSTITIONS

There has always been a disposition to connect one's personality with colors. People are supposed not only to have a fortunate number but a lucky hue as well. Planets have a certain hue, and a person's color chart agrees with that of his star.

Modern scientific research has proved the importance of color in a curative sense. No matter whether your native color is red or blue, it is a fact that the color of your wall paper may have a beneficial or harmful effect on you if you are ill.

Color undoubtedly has an influence on mental conditions.

Infusoria and the lower forms of life develop faster under one kind of color than under another, red and yellow being most favorable. Flies, ants and other insects die under the effect of blue or violet light. Why then should color not also have its influence on man?

Insane people have been cured by placing them in a room that was flooded with light of a certain color that corresponded with their aura. Blue light was thought particularly efficacious for melancholy people.

The following beliefs are current in regard to colors:

Red governs love, affection or lust.
Scarlet rules emotion and anger.
Crimson is the color of animal passion.
Bright red gives courage and confidence.
Orange is the color of simplicity or ignorance.
Brown is the hue of worldly wisdom.
Yellow, of jealousy and silliness.

In the Bible, sin is supposed to be scarlet in color, hence that color is to be avoided by virtuous people.

The devil, as the incarnation of sin, is always represented as dressed in scarlet.

Yellow and gold, according to some philosophers, correspond to the intellectual, red to the sensual, and blue to the spiritual, moral and religious nature of man.

White is the color of innocence, hence brides dress in white.

Black is the color of mourning in European and American nations, but white is the mourning hue in oriental countries.

Purple was considered the color of royalty in ancient days, probably on account of its former scarcity and expensiveness. It is also used for second mourning, as being a compromise between black and gay colors.

There is a belief that every jealous person had green eyes. This idea no doubt was formed by the fact that some people's eyes become phosphorescent under great emotion.

CHAPTER XI
PLANT SUPERSTITIONS

Quaking grass, also called maidenhair, if brought into the house brings bad luck.

If mandrake is turned up in one's garden it should be burnt at once. Many strange beliefs centre about this root. Some believe it will cause blindness if looked at too long.

To pick flowers before they are full blown, is said to cause a stye.

March marigolds will cause drinking habits if looked at too long.

If poppies are held to the eyes, it is believed they will blind one.

Primroses should not be brought into a house where there are laying hens, or the chickens will not hatch out.

CHAPTER XII
BIRD AND INSECT SUPERSTITIONS

Owls are considered unlucky birds. Their hoarse and repellent voice is a bad omen and means coming disaster.

Chaucer says: "The owl brings tidings of death."

History tells that an owl once flew into the city of Rome and as a result the place was purified and sacrifices offered to propitiate the gods and avert trouble.

Before the death of the Roman emperor, Antoninus, an owl was observed to sit over his chamber door.

The Actian War was foretold by owls flying into the Temple of Concord in Rome.

In the Middle Ages the screeching of owls was supposed to foretell plague or other calamities.

Ravens were considered equally unlucky. To have a raven fly into one's bedroom foretold disaster. The celebrated poem by Poe, "The Raven," has this belief for its motive.

Robins are considered lucky birds and it is

bad to kill one. The farmers believe that they will avert poor crops.

The high esteem in which the robin is held probably originated from the story of the "Babes in the Wood" who were covered up with leaves by the robin redbreasts after they were left to starve by their cruel guardian.

The cuckoo has long been considered as a bird of bad omen, if it enters one's home; but to hear a cuckoo cry in the woods is a good sign.

Boys take their money out of their pockets and spit on it for luck when they hear a cuckoo cry. It is a bad sign not to have any money in your pocket when you hear the cuckoo's first cry in spring.

A white bird or a crow flying against a window by night, foretells a death in the house within a year.

A robin is a bringer of good luck if it flies into the house.

Magpies have different meanings according to the number that fly about. "One for sorrow, two for mirth, three for a wedding, four for a birth, five for silver, six for gold, seven a secret that dare not be told."

To avert the evil influence of magpies, make a cross with the foot for every one in sight.

It is unlucky to look into an owl's nest.

It is a bad omen to kill a swallow or a wren or take their eggs.

Martins and swallows are God's teachers and scholars and must not be annoyed.

INSECT OMENS

It is unlucky to kill a spider. If you wish to thrive, let the spider stay alive.

A spider's web, encountered on the road should not be disturbed.

A little red ant, if it crawls into the pocket, brings money.

Crickets are considered harbingers of luck; but in some countries the contrary holds good.

To kill a red ant, brings rain.

Bees swarming on a house means that some one will die there.

If you see a black snail, throw it over your head for luck.

To kill a toad will make the bees swarm.

BEES

When putting bees into a new hive, one must knock three times on top of the old hive and tell them; otherwise they will sting you.

SIGNS, OMENS AND SUPERSTITIONS

If any one dies in a house where bees are kept, they must be told, otherwise they will stop gathering honey and die too.

In some country hives are turned around when a member of the family dies, otherwise the bees will also die.

Bees are supposed to have a religious nature and to be subject to the emotions of their owners.

In Yorkshire there is a custom of watching the hives on Christmas Eve. The people profess to be able to tell by the humming noise the bees make whether the holiday is to be a joyful one or not.

Bees have often been used for divination and the size of the swarm and the general behavior of the bees prophesies good or bad crops.

If a hive of bees dies out, it is a sign of a coming bad harvest and the farmer looks for another place to ply his profession.

To be stung by a bee, if not followed by a swelling, is a sign of coming fortune.

If three bees alight upon you at one time, it is a sign that your plans will meet with success.

CHAPTER XIII
ANIMAL PORTENTS

The following are believed to foretell death: Rats leaving a house; a hare or white rabbit crossing your path; a cow lowing three times in your face; a shrewmouse running over your foot.

It is unlucky to keep a kitten born in May. It should be drowned, as a May cat is supposed to suck a child's breath.

Goslings hatched in May bring no luck to the owner.

It is unlucky to bid a price for an animal that is not for sale. The animal is apt to die within a month.

To covet another's beast will bring you bad luck.

If a pig is killed while the moon is waning, it will be unprofitable and the bacon will shrink in the pot.

A gray horse brings good luck. Spit on the little finger and rub it on the horse, and money will come to you.

If you see a young spring lamb with the head towards you, it means good fortune.

It foretells bad luck if rats gnaw one's clothing.

It is unlucky to kill a cricket. These insects were esteemed by the ancients as a symbol of hospitality. Their singing was often used to foretell good or bad events.

A hare crossing the path of a traveller is a sign of bad fortune. A white hare, however, is regarded as a good sign.

A pig appearing to a traveller is a good sign. If a sow be accompanied by a litter of pigs, it denotes a successful trip.

The tail of a lizard is considered a lucky mascot in France, just as is the hind leg of a rabbit in this country.

To meet a white horse is considered unlucky unless the person spits at it to avert trouble.

To meet a white horse indicates that you will soon see a red-haired girl.

Rooks are believed to foretell death by leaving the house near which they have built their nests.

Killing a spider is considered unlucky. Small spiders, called "money-spinners," indicate good luck, and their webs are not to be destroyed.

If black ants appear in a house it is a sign of good luck, but red ants bring misfortune.

To meet a goat unexpectedly is bad luck; ~~to meet a sheep is a good sign.~~

HOWLING OF DOGS

The howling of dogs has always been considered a sign of coming disaster. Dogs are supposed to have a peculiar sense of coming trouble. In case of sickness, a dog is supposed to foretell the outcome.

An old writer says: "As odd and unaccountable as it may seem, dogs scent death even before it seizes a person.

In the "Odyssey," the dogs of Eumæus are described as terrified at the sight of Minerva though she was invisible to human eyes.

The howling of dogs is believed to presage death, especially in houses where some one is lying ill.

When dogs tremble and wallow upon the earth it is a sign of wind and storm.

Horses and cattle are often supposed to have this trait in common with dogs. Their keen sense of smell, or perhaps some sense which mortals do not possess, enables them to discover illness and danger.

BLACK CATS

There are conflicting beliefs regarding the influence of black cats. Some consider them a sure sign of good luck, others regard them with dread and awe.

A black cat without a single white hair is lucky, particularly if it comes to you unsolicited.

If you start out to undertake any new work or to hunt and a black cat crosses your path, you will be very lucky in your undertaking.

If you try to coax a black cat to come and he runs away, you will be disappointed in your results.

To kill a black cat is very unlucky, and means misfortune for a year.

Among Egyptians, cats were regarded with religious awe. They were mummified and buried in the graves with human beings.

Witches had a fondness for black cats, and used them in their divinations. In soothsaying, cats have always played an important role.

The brain of a black cat was considered an important ingredient in the recipes and prescriptions of the witches in the Middle Ages.

The meowing of a black cat at midnight is a bad omen, and foretells a death.

CHAPTER XIV

METEOROLOGICAL BELIEFS

To walk under a rainbow is supposed to be unlucky, as the light of a rainbow, while good in itself, harms the one it shines on.

To be out in a sunshower is good luck, and whatever you venture in that hour will be successful.

Thunder and lightning are both lucky and unlucky according to the direction from which they come.

An even number of thunder reports in quick succession have no effect, but an uneven number will bring luck.

The ancients considered thunder as an indication that Jove was angry.

Thunder from a cloudless sky, is considered an indication of luck.

To see a new moon for the first time after a change on the right-hand side or directly in front of you betokens good luck, but to see it behind you on your left, is a bad omen.

To begin a journey or other important work in

the last quarter of the moon is bad, and the venture will be a failure.

To see the new moon through a window for the first time, indicates bad luck.

The new moon seen over the right shoulder brings good fortune, over the left shoulder means failure, and straight ahead of you denotes good luck till the end of the season.

The Friday on which the new moon first appears is a bad day and Sunday is equally unfavorable for a full moon.

Red ants swarming through the earth, indicate coming of rain.

If it rains on St. Swithin's Day, it will rain for forty days more.

If the hedgehog emerges from his hole on Michaelmas and sees his shadow, prepare for thirty days more of winter.

WEATHER SIGNS AND PORTENTS

Small fleecy clouds of "curdled" appearance, indicate neither long wet nor long dry. Long streaky clouds, indicate fair weather.

Thick bands of clouds across the west, indicate stormy weather.

A "weather breeder" is a fine, warm day out

of season and foretells bad weather in the near future.

Streaks of light radiating out of clouds behind the sun foretell rain. The sun is said to be sucking up moisture.

"The moon on her back holds water in her lap."

A halo around the moon indicates rain. The bigger the wheel, the nearer the moisture.

If the evening star is in front of the moon, look out for rain.

When a guinea fowl or peacock calls, prepare for rain.

The call of the green woodpecker is a sign of rain.

Rooks gathering in large numbers and flying in a circle, foretell rain.

If it rains on Friday, it will surely rain on the next Sunday.

Shooting of corns or the aching of an old wound foretell rain.

If during the harvest a rake is carried with its teeth up, it will be a wet harvest.

When the cat scratches the leg of the table, sneezes, draws her paw over her forehead in washing her face or frisks about the house, it is a sure sign of rain.

The following are indications of rain: When crickets chirp louder than usually, when a rooster flies on the gate and crows, when a dog eats grass, and when snails are abundant.

"Wind in the east is good neither for man or beast.

Wind in the west suits everybody best."

When the robins sing high in the tree, the weather will be fine, but if they sing low down, it will rain soon.

Sea gulls on land bring rain.

"Red sky at night, shepherd's delight.

Red sky in the morning, shepherd's warning."

Early mist indicates a fine day.

If ice will bear a man before Christmas, it will not bear a mouse afterwards.

If the sun shines through the apple trees on Christmas, it foretells a fine crop of apples.

"If in February there be no rain,

The hay won't prosper nor the grain."

All other months of the year curse a fine February.

If a cat lies in the sun in February, she will creep under the grate in March.

"When the oak comes before the ash, summer will be dry and mash."

"Rain on Good Friday and Easter Day, brings lots of grass but little hay."

Cold May, short hay! Leaky June, plenty of corn!

If it rains on St. Swithin's Day, the apples are christened and the early kind may be picked.

Warm October means a cold February.

Snow that lingers will bring more snow.

COMETS AND METEORS

That the sudden appearance of a big star with a long tail should cause fear and apprehension is but natural. Primitive man, in fact until a few decades ago, saw in the fiery celestial visitor a sure omen of disaster. In religious countries in the Middle Ages, the appearance of a comet was associated with the second coming of Christ.

In the year 1712, Whiston, a clergyman and astronomer, predicted the appearance of a comet and stated that the world would be destroyed by fire a few days thereafter. The comet appeared punctually according to his calculations, and the inhabitants of England began to prepare for the end of the world. People got into boats believing that the water was the safest place. Divine service was held in all churches, and rich men parted with their wealth. The comet left without having accomplished any damage.

Comets have often been regarded as the precursor of war and famine and nearly every big war occurred soon after the appearance of a comet.

Although we know now that comets are harmless things, and rarely trouble the earth, superstition still clings to them.

Special prayers were instituted by various popes to nullify the evil a comet might do. In Catholic countries these are still used as a preventive of trouble.

It is considered unlucky to engage in any new business during the continuation of a comet in the sky.

Children born during a comet will have a difficult time of it, and are subject to sudden death.

Shooting stars or meteors have also been the subject of many strange beliefs. When a shooting star flashes across the sky, wish for money, and you will be sure to get it.

A sick person, seeing a shooting star, will recover within a month.

If you set out on a voyage at night and see a shooting star, your trip will be successful.

Lovers seeing shooting stars and wishing for health, wealth or happiness, will have their wish gratified.

CHAPTER XV
VOCATIONAL SUPERSTITIONS
SUPERSTITIONS OF KINGS

King Harold of England considered Saturday his lucky day.

According to Celtic chronicles, each king of Scotland had some favorite day, and was forbidden by the astrologers of his reign from doing certain things on designated days.

The kings of Ireland were not allowed to have the sun fall on their beds at Tara Castle.

The King of Munster was forbidden to have a feast at Killarney from Monday to the end of the week.

The King of Connaught believed it ill luck to wear a speckled garment or to ride a speckled horse.

The King of Ulster would not go to certain parts of his kingdom during March for fear of disaster.

October 14th was supposed to be a lucky day for the kings of England.

The sixth of April was a lucky day for Alexander the Great. On that day he conquered Darius and won a great sea battle.

The sixth of April was also lucky for Alexander's father, Phillip of Macedon. On that day he captured Potidæa, his general overthrew the Illyrians, and his horse won at the Olympian games.

The month of January has been unlucky for kings. Charles I was beheaded that month. Napoleon III and King Victor Emmanuel of Italy died in January.

King Louis XVI of France found the 21st an important day. On April 21st, 1770, he was married, and every great event of his reign occurred on that day. On January 21st, 1793, he was beheaded.

Cromwell considered the 3rd of September as his lucky day. He gained several great victories on that date.

The Duke of Monmouth was told by a fortuneteller that if he survived St. Swithin's Day he would be a great man. He died on that day.

Napoleon Bonaparte considered Friday his unlucky day and Monday his fortunate day.

Henry IV of France considered Friday lucky

SIGNS, OMENS AND SUPERSTITIONS

and preferred to undertake important things on that day.

The late Emperor of Austria was superstitious and attributed all his family troubles to a curse that was launched against him by a countess who believed herself injured by him.

The Hohenzollern family, of which the kaiser is the most talked-of member, have their pet superstitions, one of them being that the apparition of a woman in white betokens the death of one of the family.

CARD PLAYERS' SUPERSTITIONS

Luck plays such an important part with gamblers and card players that it is not surprising they have a multitude of beliefs and superstitions. Where every move is connected with blind chance and skill is entirely secondary, every detail of the game is watched for some sign of import or some omen that will bring success. Here are some of the many beliefs that are current in English-speaking countries:

To play cards on a table without a cover is considered unlucky.

A green cover is the most fortunate to play on.

To lend money to an adversary with which to

play is unlucky. To borrow money during a game is lucky.

In Monte Carlo and other gambling places there is a belief that after a suicide of an unlucky player, all those playing against the bank will win. When the news of a suicide becomes known, therefore, the card rooms at once fill with eager players.

If you wish a friend to win at cards, stick a pin in the lapel of his coat.

To drop a card on the floor during a game is a bad sign, and means the loss of that game.

Singing, while playing, is a sign that your side will lose.

To have another person look over your shoulder while playing, or put his foot on the rung of your chair, is a forerunner of bad luck.

To play at the same table with a cross-eyed man is a sign that you will lose.

To lose your temper or get into a passion over the game is a sign of a loss.

The four of clubs is an unlucky card to get. It is called the devil's bedstead.

It helps your luck to keep the chips carefully stacked up before you.

Most players have their own private superstitions based on past experiences. A certain hand

SIGNS, OMENS AND SUPERSTITIONS

always foretells good luck, while the cards coming in a certain order may mean the reverse.

Winning the first game often means that you will win the third. Holding your cards in a certain way brings success.

Playing on certain days is unlucky for some, lucky for others. To play before 6 P. M. on Fridays is unlucky.

Turning one's chair around three times is often resorted to to change one's luck.

Playing with a fresh deck of cards is another way of forcing the goddess of fortune to be propitious.

Most players have a lucky card which they touch with the index finger before sitting down to play. This insures good fortune.

ACTORS' SUPERSTITIONS

Actors may be counted among the most superstitious people in the world. Their success depends upon so many unforeseen contingencies, and so many elements enter into their enterprises, that they look with awe and misgiving upon every trivial incident. In different countries they have different rites and beliefs, but the following seem to be the most prevalent in English-speaking lands:

Whistling in a theatre is a sign of very bad luck, and there is no offense that is more quickly frowned upon by the manager. It was formerly difficult for a vaudeville artist who made a specialty of whistling in his act to get an engagement.

It is considered bad luck to change the costume in which an actor first made his success in a piece. In cases of a long run the garment is often worn until it becomes threadbare.

The witches' song in Macbeth is believed to have an uncanny power for evil, and many actors cannot be induced to play in that tragedy.

To repeat the last lines of a play at rehearsals is considered an ill omen.

The pictures of an ostrich or peacock are considered unlucky.

To turn the handle of the wrong door in seeking a manager or play-broker is considered very unlucky. To ward against failure, the applicant must return home and start out afresh next day.

Yellow is an unlucky color for an actor. The color of one's costume often creates a loss of memory while learning a part.

The looping of a drop curtain is a sure forerunner of evil.

Wigs bring luck, and many an actor wears one although his part does not call for it.

If an actor's shoes squeak on making his entrance it is a sign that he will have the applause of the audience.

If an actor kicks off his shoes and they alight on their soles, it is a good omen; but if they fall on their sides, it is a bad sign.

Cats are considered very lucky by actors, and to have a cat run across the stage during a rehearsal is considered very lucky. It brings bad luck to kick a cat.

To have a person look over the actor's shoulder while he is making up and looking at himself in the glass is unlucky.

To stumble over anything in making an entrance is bad, and will cause him to fail in his lines.

If his costume catches in the scenery as he enters he must go back and make a new entrance or else have bad luck during the act.

The peep-hole through which the actor looks out at the audience is usually in the centre, as either side may bring bad luck.

THEATRE SUPERSTITIONS

Managers have their pet superstitions as well as actors.

To accept a play that has not been refused by at least one manager is considered by some as a sign of failure.

If the first purchaser of seats for a performance is an old man or old woman it means that the play will have a long run. A young person means the reverse.

To receive a torn bank note for a ticket is a bad sign for the box office man, and means a loss of position. A big bill for which he must make change is a good omen.

If an usher seats a person in seat thirteen or a multiple thereof, he will have bad luck.

An usher considers it bad luck to have a lady tip him for a program, but a gentleman's tip insures good luck.

The first tip of the season is briskly rubbed on the leg of the usher's trousers and then kept in his pocket as a lucky piece.

To receive a smile from an actor over the footlights is a good omen.

A woman fainting in a theatre is considered a

bad sign and means that the play will come to a speedy end.

A death in a playhouse during a performance is a certain hoodoo, and usually ends in an unexpected termination of the run of the play.

COMMERCIAL TRAVELLERS' SUPERSTITIONS

Travelling men, whose lives are a constant struggle after orders, are apt to consider trifles as an index of coming fortune, or the reverse, and many are their peculiar beliefs.

When, on starting out, a drummer finds he has forgotten his order book, he will take no orders till it is sent after him.

A necktie worn when the first order is taken is often worn till the end of the trip, as it brings good luck. With some, the suit takes the place of the tie.

A salesman often goes into a stranger's store and tries to sell a bill before tackling his own regular customer. He believes that if he is turned down by one, he will be sure to sell the right man.

A flock of sheep seen on starting out is a good sign. A pig or drove of pigs is even better.

If no order has been taken for several days, the conscientious traveller will rest up for a day, take a bath and change his clothes for a change of luck.

Muttering some incantation or wish while a difficult customer is making up his mind is often resorted to.

A lucky pocket-piece twirled in the left hand is supposed to insure an order where the customer is undecided.

A horseshoe carried in the bottom of a sample trunk is supposed to insure success during the trip.

DRESSMAKERS AND SEAMSTRESSES

Seamstresses have a code of beliefs of their own, many of which are curious.

To prick a finger and draw blood while sewing a bride's dress bodes ill for the bride's married life. To stain the dress with blood means an early death for the wearer.

To try on a bride's dress by the seamstress and wear it for an hour before the bride wears it betokens an engagement for the seamstress.

To lose a thimble while making a bride's dress means exceptionally good luck for the bride.

To be employed to make a mourning outfit for a young widow betokens an early marriage for the seamstress.

To turn the material on the wrong side and sew it thus by mistake so that the dress will have to be ripped and resewn means good luck for the wearer.

To drop your scissors on the floor means a visitor who will bring welcome news. Should the scissors break, it means a keen disappointment.

To sew with the wrong colored silk or thread by mistake is a sign of bad luck for the wearer unless the work is ripped and sewn over.

To make an all white dress is always productive of luck.

A spot of dirt or oil on a new dress where it will show means disappointment for the wearer.

It was formerly considered unlucky for a bride to help sew her own wedding dress.

SAILORS' SUPERSTITIONS

The sea is one of the greatest marvels of creation, and perhaps the most mysterious. It is full of dangers, and from time immemorial has been the subject of many superstitions. It is natural that sailors should attach a meaning to everything that promises a safe voyage.

The sea is supposed to be filled with monsters that cause no end of trouble if they are not propitiated by some rite. A fleet on the sea drives away these monsters.

A sailing vessel is supposed to sail faster when running from an enemy than otherwise.

By speaking to his sailing vessel as he would to a horse, many an old salt believes he gets greater speed.

A kingfisher hanged by a nail to the mast is used to prophesy the direction of the wind.

When a great auk, an aquatic bird, appears, sailors believe they will have a speedy voyage. If the bird settles on deck it is a good omen.

Seeing three magpies predicts a successful voyage. One magpie, however, is a sign of bad luck.

A seal is considered a lucky omen, and it is wicked to kill one.

An albatross brings good luck and creates favorable winds. To kill an albatross is an omen of very bad luck. This is portrayed in the "Rime of the Ancient Mariner."

SIGNS, OMENS AND SUPERSTITIONS

A dove alighting on a ship is a sign of favorable winds.

Dolphins and porpoises playing about a ship presage a storm.

An eight-arm cuttlefish is regarded by sailors as a bad omen.

Barnacles that cling to a ship are believed to change into birds after the vessel has been on a cruise for six months.

French sailors dread the nocturnal visits of a sort of mischievous Puck or sprite who is supposed to play pranks while they sleep.

An appeal to the Virgin is supposed by Latin sailors to calm a storm at sea.

Sailing on Friday is considered bad luck. Steamers do not now fear this day as much as formerly.

When a Chinese junk is ready to go to sea, priests are invited to go on board to chant a prayer and offer a sacrifice to Tien How, the god of the sea. Gongs and drums are beaten.

A shark following a ship is looked upon as a sure sign of death of one of the passengers or crew.

When a storm arises and a vessel is in danger it is supposed that a sinful person is on board and causes the trouble. This belief grew out of the story of Jonah.

Most sailors make the sign of the cross before launching a boat in an angry sea.

Christening new ships is a relic of an ancient rite when wine was offered to Neptune as a propitiatory sacrifice to insure his favor.

The custom of blessing a ship is an old one and is supposed to keep a ship from harm.

Carrying dead bodies on shipboard is regarded with superstitious dread by sailors, and those that die during a voyage are usually buried at sea.

FISHERMEN'S SUPERSTITIONS

During oyster dredging, fishermen often keep up a monotonous chant to charm the oysters into their net. This has given rise to the following verse, reprinted from an old book on fishermen's lore:

"The herring loves the merry moonlight,
The mackerel loves the wind;
But the oyster loves the dredger's song,
For he comes of gentle kind."

Norwegian fishermen perform a sort of sacred rite before going on the hunt for herring. They drink a "white lug," a sort of toddy. They believe it insures a big catch.

In many countries fishermen are afraid to assist a drowning man for fear that the water sprite will be offended and drive the fish from the nets.

Burmese fishermen offer fruit and rice to "Nat," the spirit of the water, otherwise he will scare away the fish.

Many fishermen believe that spitting on the bait before casting the hook will make the catch certain.

Portuguese fishermen during a storm attach an image of St. Anthony to the mast and pray to it. If that don't help, they curse and beat the image to make it behave and do their behests.

It is considered lucky to throw the first fish caught back into the water to induce other fish to come to the hook.

TURFMEN'S SUPERSTITIONS

Men who follow the races and make their living on the turf are in the same category as card players and gamblers. Their winnings depend exclusively on chance, and it is easy to understand how they invest every occurrence with some mysterious meaning and believe that certain signs or omens will bring good or bad luck. Some of their superstitions are childish, but their belief in them often brings the desired results.

On the way to the races, if a turfman sees a name like that of the horse that is run that day, he takes it for an omen that the horse will win.

The initials of names on signboards or the headlines in the paper he is reading are all made to do service in spelling the name of the horse that is to be victorious.

To meet a funeral on the way to the track is a bad omen, although an empty hearse denotes good luck.

To dream of a horse that is entered for a race is lucky, but it will not win the first time it is run. It is sure to win the second time, however, and it is safe to bet on it then.

To meet a cross-eyed man on the way to the track is very bad, but to meet a cross-eyed woman is lucky. A cross-eyed negro foretells the best kind of luck.

To meet a black cat brings bad luck, while a white cat is excellent. To be followed by a strange dog is a good sign. To see a piebald horse means success.

To give alms to a blind beggar brings good luck and to touch the hump of a hunchback man is a sure sign of success.

When the saddle girth of a horse gets loose and the jockey is obliged to get off and tighten it, it is a sure bet that the horse will win.

Money that is won should be carried loose in the pocket, and not in a purse or wallet. It will then pave the way for more.

To find money on the track is a bad thing. It should be given away in charity.

BASEBALL SUPERSTITIONS

Baseball players have a curious code of beliefs, which differ with nearly every team. They have their mascots, that are supposed to bring them good luck, and stand in awe of the "jinx" that often defeats their best plans.

When a team runs behind in its score a change of pitcher or catcher often retrieves their chances.

It is unlucky to play with a bat that is split, even if the damage is slight. A new bat must be procured.

If on the way to the game any name is encountered that suggests the name of one of the teams, that team will be successful.

If any part of a player's uniform is missing or torn, it means bad luck for the team.

A cross-eyed umpire is tabooed as a hoodoo.

To have a "southpaw," or left-handed pitcher, brings good luck to the team.

It is a common belief that the team losing the first innings will win the game at the end.

WAITERS' SUPERSTITIONS

Waiters, depending as they must upon chance tips, are very prone to be superstitious, and have developed a series of rites and ceremonies that are supposed to bring them the coveted fee.

Drawing out a chair for the customer to seat himself is sure to bring a good-sized fee. If the customer for any reason takes a different seat from that indicated it is a bad omen.

A certain arrangement of knife and fork is sure to produce a good result. The fork must lie near the plate and the knife on the outside and parallel. Any other arrangement is bad.

Opening up the napkin for the customer is a good sign.

To bring a customer a second portion of butter before he asks for it is good. If a customer sends out a dish for any reason, it means bad luck for the rest of the day.

To receive a big tip early in the day is a bad sign. All the rest of the tips are apt to be small.

To break a dish is a very bad omen. It means not only loss of wages, but the loss of tips as well.

If a waiter finds that a certain salutation results in a tip, he must use the same salutation on all clients during the day.

To wait on a hunchback customer is a sign of good luck and results in a good inflow of tips. To wait on a one-armed man is bad.

CHAPTER XVI
MISCELLANEOUS
PORTENTS OF EVIL

Furniture creaking at night without visible cause, is a sign of death or illness.

Letters crossing in the mail betoken evil fortune.

When the church bell strikes while the parson is giving out his text, some one in the congregation will die.

Ringing sounds in the ear foretell trouble.

Three people making up a bed is a bad sign, and foretells illness to one of them.

The ticking of a "death tick," a minute insect that lives in wood, is a sign of coming trouble.

BREAKING FRIENDSHIP

When poker and tongs hang both on the same side of the fireplace it betokens a breaking of friendship.

Passing a friend on the stairs, foretells a rupture.

When two persons kindle a fire together, it foretells that they will soon quarrel.

Two persons washing their hands in the same basin or using the same towel at the same time, had better beware, for their friendship will be of short duration.

In all of the above cases, making a cross with the thumb will prevent the evil from being carried out.

DRINKING TOASTS

Drinking to the health of a friend is a very old custom and goes back to the beginning of civilization. The Roman gallant would drink as many glasses as there were letters in the name of his sweetheart.

The origin of the word "toast" is uncertain. An old writer claims that in the reign of Charles the Second, a piece of toasted bread was dropped in the wine, and that a wit, seeing that the wine had all been quaffed, remarked: "If I can't drink the wine, I can at least have the toast."

To give or drink a toast signifies to offer a sentiment in honor of some dear person, and wish him or her good health. It is supposed to be efficacious.

The ancients poured wine upon the ground in honor of the gods. The modern feaster prefers to pour it into himself in honor of his friends. Many a man drinks to the health of others and forgets about his own health.

To break a glass while drinking a toast is a bad omen, and may result in the early death of the person toasted.

To spill wine while drinking a toast is a good omen, and brings health and happiness to the one concerned.

PIOUS EJACULATIONS

The custom of qualifying an assertion or a wish with some pious remark in order to avert trouble, is well-nigh universal and was as prevalent among the ancients as with us.

The Romans, whenever they told of their intended movements or of anything they expected to accomplish in the future, always prefixed their remarks with *"Deo Volente,"* or some similar words.

The modern American says, "God willing," when he tells of something he expects to do. This is supposed to remove any hoodoo that may interfere with his anticipated deed.

SIGNS, OMENS AND SUPERSTITIONS 153

Similarly the German says, *"So Gott will."* The Frenchman says, *"A Dieu ne deplaise,"* and so every language has its equivalent.

In speaking about the possibility of anything evil happening to one's dear ones, it is customary to say, "God forbid."

In discussing the merits or deeds of one's wife or other dear relative, we often say "God bless her or him," which is supposed to remove any occult influence for evil.

Jews, when discussing the good points or praiseworthy traits of their dear ones, say, *"Unbeschrien,"* which literally means "without wishing to praise." This prevents the praise from reacting and becoming a reproach.

In speaking of their dead, the Germans often add the word *"selig"* to the name. This means "blessed" or of "blessed memory," and is equivalent to saying, "Peace to his ashes."

The English expressions of "Dear me," "My goodness" and "Goodness gracious," are really modifications of *"dio mio,"* "My God," "Gracious God," etc., and had their origin in the desire to call on the Deity to bring comfort or help. So also "Hully Gee" is a corruption of "Holy Jesus."

The Europeans think nothing of interjecting the

name of the Deity into their ordinary conversation. *"Mein Gott," "Act Gott," "Mon Dieu,"* etc., take place of our "Dear me," etc. They are not used in the spirit of blasphemy, but as pious words to avert evil.

Many people before starting out on any errand, or even before entering a room, say to themselves, "Good luck," or other phrase, in the nature of a silent prayer.

Birthday wishes, festival wishes and congratulations are all related to this same class of prayers or pious wishes, and are supposed to influence the mysterious power that rules the universe, to send its best gifts and to keep away harm.

CHAPTER XVII
SUPERSTITIONS OF THE ORTHODOX JEWS

The following is a list of some of the most common beliefs of the orthodox Hebrews. Many of them have their original in some Biblical quotation or in some interpretation of a Biblical text. This collection is taken from the pages of the "Jewish Encyclopedia."

Animal:—To see an animal in an unexpected place indicates the finding of a treasure.

Bachelor:—Bachelors are not looked on with favor. As it is not good to be alone, every man is supposed to marry. Sand is strewn before the hearse when a bachelor is buried, as a reproach.

Barrenness:—To cure barrenness, water was prescribed in which moss taken from the Temple wall in Jerusalem was cooked.

Bat:— To kill a bat with a gold coin was considered lucky.

Bathtub:— A child's bathtub was not to be used for any other purpose, or the child would meet with misfortune.

Bear:— To eat a bear's heart would convert the eater into a tyrant.

Bed:— It is considered lucky for girls to sit on a bride's bed, and will cause other marriages.

Blood:— As blood was supposed to carry the life of the animal and was used on the altar, it is not eaten by professing Jews.

Blood as a cure:— For many illnesses, blood was smeared on the breast and forehead. The blood of a rooster was usually taken for this purpose.

Bone:— When a fishbone has been swallowed, place another fishbone on the head, and the offending bone will be either ejected or swallowed completely.

Book:— It is dangerous to go away and leave a book open.

Bread:— After saying the usual blessing over bread at a meal (grace), the bread should be cut in two before eating.

Bride:— If on the return from the marriage canopy, the bride takes the groom's hand, she will be the ruling power in the family. If the groom takes the bride's hand, he will be boss.

Broom:— A table should never be brushed off with a broom, as it may bring poverty.

Brothers:— It is unlucky for three married brothers to live in the same town.

Buckets:— It is unlucky to come across an empty bucket in going out of a house, or a full bucket in coming in.

Cat:— When a cat licks her paws, be prepared for company.

Convulsions:— When a child has convulsions, break an earthenware pot in front of its face, to drive away the demon.

Cemetery:— In order to allay the fears of any member of a community of being the first to be buried in a new cemetery, a rooster is often slaughtered and buried.

Curse:— An undeserved curse, usually rebounds on the one who curses, and brings him bad luck.

Dead:— A dead person is supposed to know what is going on until the last spade-full of earth is placed on his grave.

Dirt:— It is unlucky to throw dirt after a man who is leaving a house.

Eggs:— To steal an egg brings poverty.

Epidemics:— In case of an epidemic, never open the door of your home to any one until he has knocked three times.

Evil Eye:— To avert the curse of the evil eye,

spit three times on your finger tips and make a quick movement with your hand through the air.

Eye:— If the right eye itches, rejoice; if the left, you will grieve.

Fingers:— When washing the fingers, hold them downwards so that the water will drip off. Evil spirits will depart with the water.

Feet:— Itching of the feet denotes that you will make a voyage to a place you have never been to.

Hair:— If child's hair is cut on certain days, an elflock will grow.

Looking back:— In running from danger, never look back, or like Lot's wife, you will come to grief.

Money:— In taking money out of a purse or box, always leave a coin, however small, as a luck token.

Money:— Dreaming of money is a sign of bad luck.

Mourning:— Don't weep too long for the departed or you may have to weep for some one else. Weep three days, mourn seven, and refrain from wearing jewelry for thirty days.

Oven:— It is unlucky to leave an oven empty. When you are not baking in it, keep a piece of

SIGNS, OMENS AND SUPERSTITIONS

wood within, or you may not have anything to bake.

Rats:— If rats leave one house for another, it is a sign of bad luck for the first and good luck for the second.

Shoes:— Never walk out with only one shoe or slipper on your foot. It may forecast a death.

Shroud:— In making a shroud, avoid knots.

Sisters:— Two sisters should not marry on the same day, nor should two brothers marry two sisters. Both bring bad luck.

Sweeping:— It is unlucky to sweep out a room at night, or to throw sweepings into the street after sundown.

Widowhood:— The fourth husband of a widow will die soon after his marriage.

Spitting:— When a person spits at another, he takes over the other's sins.

Travelling:— Monday is a bad day for travelling, but Tuesday is a lucky day.